Fear
and
Smear

Books by Pat Anderson

The McGlinchy Code
The Crimes of Miss Jane Goldie
Only The Good
Torrent
Clash of the Agnivores
A Toast to Charlie Hanrahan

For children

The Skyscraper Rocket Ship
The Ceremony at Goreb Ridge
The Brain Thing
The Football Star

Mighty Pete and the School Bully
School
Mighty Pete and the Trainer Train
Trainers

Fear and Smear

THE CAMPAIGN AGAINST SCOTTISH INDEPENDENCE

Pat Anderson

Snowy Publications MMXV

Dedicated to 'The 45'.

CONTENTS

Preface

Cards on the table; I voted YES in the Scottish independence referendum. That might make me biased but I have tried my best not to be. I cannot, however, say the same for most of my sources. Practically every newspaper was on the side of maintaining the Union and many feel that the broadcast media were too. Online media and blogs balanced things by being on the side of independence. It was virtually impossible to find any source that was completely detached from the debate; I had to tease things out carefully. Hopefully I succeeded.

I had sworn that I would not tackle a book like this again. It is much easier to write fiction, where the hardest thing is trying to think up names for your characters. 'Clash of the Agnivores' involved months of research and I promised myself that I would not put my poor brain through that again, unless it was for that PhD I have always been meaning to do!

It probably makes it even harder when you have studied for a degree in History; you feel that you have to justify practically every statement and will venture no opinion unless there are verifiable sources to back it up. This means that if you think a thing happened for a particular reason you have to spend hours looking for something to back it up. Often you can find nothing and have to abandon that line of thought entirely.

Mick, on Bampots Utd, almost dared me to do this book and I decided to rise to the challenge. I will leave it to you to decide if I have wasted my time or not! Perhaps I had better refrain from saying 'Never again' this time; 'Clash of the Agnivores' is crying out for a sequel!

Again, I am using the excuse that this is a short book to explain the lack of an index. Perhaps you might forgive me if you realise that I not only wrote this book but edited it, formatted it, tried to makes sure that it actually looks like a professionally-produced book and designed the cover.

As usual, thanks go to all Bampots for their support – even Monti and his hound! I am also grateful to (Rev.) Stuart Campbell, whose website 'Wings Over Scotland' led me down some interesting intellectual alleys. And finally, special thanks to Callum Martin for his crucial piece of digging. Who is he? You will find out in Chapter 4!

If you are reading the Kindle version of this book you might notice that I have added a few bells and whistles. The chapter titles on the Contents Page link directly to each chapter. Clicking on the title of the chapter you are in will take you back to the Contents Page.

Click on the footnote numbers and you will be taken to the appropriate reference. Clicking on the reference name will take you to the web page I used, assuming you are connected to the internet. Click on (R) to take you back to exactly where you left off in the book.

If you are reading this on a computer you might have to hold down the 'Ctrl' button while you are clicking on the links.

Introduction

There was a feeling of excitement in the air. It was what it must have felt like at the start of the American, French or even Russian Revolution. There was no dumping of tea, no Paul Revere riding with a warning, no sans-culottes storming the Bastille or troops refusing to fire on strikers. All we had to do was put a cross in a box and we could change our country just as much as those revolutionaries had done.

Amid all the bright-eyed optimism, however, there was the constant, all-pervasive feeling that something was wrong. People giving out leaflets found themselves described in the papers as 'cybernat thugs' or worse. If they were attacked or beaten up nobody wanted to know about it, least of all the media. Young people dancing to music; men, women and children demonstrating outside BBC Scotland; folk shouting back at Jim Murphy; all found themselves condemned for being bullies and trying to intimidate voters. It did not add up. The stories in the papers bore no relation at all to what was going on in the streets. Surely the media were not lying?

As it turned out, they were! It was all part-and-parcel of how the media, especially the press, portrayed those campaigning for independence. Personal insults were thrown at Alex Salmond, the SNP was accused of being a fascist organisation and independence supporters were all characterised as 'cybernats' and thugs. No slurs, of course, were allowed against those fine, upstanding chaps (and chappesses) fighting to maintain the Union. And any violence or vandalism perpetrated by Unionists was, by and large, ignored.

While accusing the SNP of running an organised campaign of intimidation, the Unionist side ran its own organised campaign of lies and disinformation. There were two main elements to this campaign: painting Alex

Salmond and the SNP in as bad a light as possible and frightening everyone half to death with tales of disappearing jobs, pensions and hospitals.

Of course, it could be argued that the same thing goes on in a general election and it most certainly does. There is an election for the Westminster Parliament coming up in 2015 and already (January 2015) the printed press is lining up on either side. We all know which party each particular newspaper supports, although for some of them we shall have to wait and see who Rupert Murdoch has decided to be friends with this time round. The television channels, meanwhile, will dissect each side's argument minutely, leaving us all even more confused.

The referendum on Scottish independence, however, was a different matter entirely. Every single newspaper in the whole UK was on one side of the debate, with the exception of the Sunday Herald. This, of course, meant there were no lies or smears against the Unionists and no scare stories about what would happen if Scotland stayed in the UK. The television, as well, did its usual examination of every detail; on this occasion, however, only one side had its arguments treated in this way.

A justification was provided for this overwhelming bias by claiming that there was no need to dissect the Unionist case, since it was just arguing for retaining the status quo. It was the independence side that wanted change, so it stood to reason that their arguments were the ones that required close examination.

This would have been a reasonable enough explanation if it was not for one thing; nobody actually presented a case for staying in the Union per se. The Unionist campaign might have called itself Better Together but, in reality, it should have been called 'Worse Apart'! The whole basis of the campaign was to tell us what a terrifying prospect awaited us if we voted YES.

So what we were presented with was two visions of an independent Scotland; one positive, one negative. Only one of these visions, however, was subjected to any scrutiny; it is unnecessary to specify which one!

Politicians like to pretend that all the personal attacks and negativity makes no difference in the end; this is especially the case if they win! They say that the electorate weighed up the options and made an informed choice. If this was really the case then why do they bother with all the negative stuff in the first place?

The fact is that very few people actually do weigh things up. We all like to think that we are immune and it is only others, perhaps not as intelligent or well-informed as ourselves, who are taken in by propaganda. The truth is, however, that we all fall for it every day. Billions of pounds are spent each year in advertising and companies would not waste this money if it did not work. We all go to the shops to buy products we have been talked into wanting, while anybody that stands, considering the merits of different packets of cornflakes is viewed as a complete nut!

Those of us that were not taken in by the propaganda of the Unionists were immune either because we had already made up our minds or because we were the sceptical types that never believe what the media tell us. Many others were rather wary of independence at first; the Unionist propaganda merely preyed on their fear.

And, essentially, that was how the NO campaign won. People are naturally wary of change, even if it will be to their advantage. A lot of folk might well have wanted to weigh things up but never got the chance; our media saw to that. So all anyone had to go on was a daily diet of fear of what might happen if they voted YES and continuous personal attacks on Alex Salmond and the SNP.

The only place to find the arguments in favour of independence was online, on social media. That possibly explains why initial demographic analyses show that the older one was, the more likely one was to vote NO.

Probably the most amazing thing about the referendum was what a close-run fight it turned out to be. With the whole power of the media against it, the independence campaign managed to get almost 45% of the voters to put their cross in the YES box. It showed the power of social media and it is unsurprising that most governments, including our own, are afraid of this new phenomenon.

And so, let us begin our look at all the black propaganda that constituted the Unionist case. We shall start by looking at the smear campaign that was waged against Alex Salmond.

Fear and Smear

BALLOT PAPER

Vote (X) ONLY ONCE

Do you agree that Scotland should be an independent country?
Do you agree to living in a one-party, Nazi state?
Do you agree to having no job and no pension?
Do you agree to having no NHS?
Do you want to live in a skint country?
Come on - The Queen said 'No!'

| YES | |
| NO | X |

1

Der Schottischereichsführer

In the campaign to keep Scotland as part of the United Kingdom, it was decided very early on to concentrate on personalities rather than policies. This was especially true of the media; it was going to be very difficult for the likes of the Daily Record to convince us all that we were Better Together while at the same time reporting on food banks and abject poverty in Scotland. It would be much easier to stick to making us believe that it was a straight choice between Westminster and Alex Salmond.

Looking back at the media coverage of the referendum campaign, it is difficult to believe that other parties and organisations were involved in calling for Scottish independence. Members of the Green Party or the Scottish Socialists were rarely interviewed in the press or on television, leaving people with the impression that it was purely an SNP campaign.

Our Fourth Estate went even further. The campaign was not about the SNP; it was about Alex Salmond. It was virtually impossible to find reports on speeches by anyone other than Salmond; even other members of the SNP were often left out. The whole emphasis was on making people believe that a tick in the YES box was a vote for Alex Salmond.

Very few brand names get to be so associated with a particular product that they are used instead of the actual name of the product; Hoover and Sellotape immediately spring to mind. Coca-Cola is almost synonymous with the U.S.A; so much so that the near-worldwide takeover by American products, music and culture is known as 'Coca-Colonisation'. Manufacturers would pay a small fortune for an advertising campaign that would make their products so ubiquitous; Alex Salmond got it for nothing.

Every day, in every newspaper, Alex Salmond's face was staring out at you. It was the same on television. His image appeared so much on the BBC that he was in serious danger of becoming the new John Barrowman. On ITV, Channel 4 and Channel 5 he was on more times than many of the well-known adverts. It became so that you could not even think of Scottish independence without imagining the face of Alex Salmond.

The power of the media to achieve this kind of association is remarkable; see Gary Lineker and you cannot help thinking of Walker's crisps. Lynda Bellingham is remembered as the Oxo mum; while for many of us William Franklyn will always be the man from Sch…You know who. To anyone that was around in the 1970s the name Patrick Allen probably means nothing. Show them a picture of the actor, however, and they will immediately recognise him as the man in the helicopter in the Barratt Homes adverts.

It works the other way round as well. Who can resist doing a Henry Cooper impersonation when they get a Brut product at Christmas? Get a pint of Fosters lager and you cannot help thinking of Paul Hogan and his 'Amber nectar'. No wonder Kevin Bridges turned down doing an advert for safe sex! Our media was doing the same with the Scottish independence referendum; mention 'referendum' and everyone would immediately picture Alex Salmond.

Eventually, Patrick Harvie, co-convenor of, and MSP for, the Green Party, had to speak up about the subject. He had to let everyone know that the referendum was not about Alex Salmond and the SNP. Unfortunately, he fell into the trap of blaming Salmond and his party for this.

'Part of the problem is the SNP's attempts to imply – quite wrongly – that a Yes vote is an endorsement of everything in their "white paper", Scotland's Future.'[1]

Of course, it could be argued that Harvie was quite right in this assessment and that it was Salmond and the SNP that were calling the shots rather than the media. After all, Patrick Harvie wrote occasional columns in the Daily Record and the Glasgow Evening Times; so surely the media were being fair in trying to represent the broad spectrum of the YES campaign?

The thing is that most people do not read opinion columns to help them make up their minds about a debate. On the contrary, if you read the online comments and letters to the papers, listen to phone-ins on the radio or venture onto Twitter, Facebook or blogs, it becomes clear that folk reacting to such articles do so from an already entrenched position. Reading or hearing someone say, 'I had no idea which way to vote but that article certainly helped me make my mind up,' is a rare occurrence indeed. Much more usual are comments like, 'I could not agree more', 'That neatly puts into words exactly how I feel' or 'Who the hell does this cockroach think he is'.

In this computer-savvy age most people are adept at using the internet and no longer rely on one hard-copy newspaper for information. Just about everybody reads the same story on multiple sites; some eager souls even pay a subscription for the privilege. We all know these days that newspapers have political agendas and we are well aware of which paper supports which party and which causes. People nowadays use online editions of newspapers and news sites, as well as television and radio, to get some semblance of truth about what is going on in the world. Most of us rely on our innate biases and prejudices to weigh up what is true and what is not; there are those, however, who keep an open mind on what the facts are. These are the people that campaigns need to target.

Those already in the YES camp would be well aware of who was involved in the campaign, since they would actively search out websites that appealed to their particular interest. Equally, those dead-set against Scottish independence would be aware for the same reasons; their opinions would be reinforced by blogs etc. that agreed with their viewpoint. Each side would also read the sites of the other side, again to strengthen its own opinion; for example, to think along the lines of, 'Oh, her! I knew it! I just knew she'd be involved!'

The supporters of both sides would know that the Green Party and the Scottish Socialists were involved in the YES campaign and would actively seek out websites where they could either offer their support or argue with them, or even jeer at them.

The campaign, therefore, was aimed at neither of these sides; it is very rare to change somebody's mind about an important matter like this. It was aimed at, as with all electoral campaigns, those in the middle; the people that had not made up their minds either way. Such folk will not look up partisan websites for their information, nor will they rely on editorials or polemical opinion columns. They depend on getting some kind of balanced view from the media, whether online or television. So what kind of balanced view did they get?

From the newspapers throughout the campaign it is virtually impossible to discern that there were others engaged in the independence campaign besides the SNP. Could anyone discover why the Green Party was supporting Scottish independence from the papers or online news sites? Or what about the Scottish Socialists; what were their reasons for campaigning for a YES vote? These parties were almost completely ignored in the rush to make us all believe that it was simply an SNP campaign.

Other organisations involved in the campaign included Women for Independence, Labour for Independence, the National Collective and Business for Scotland. During the referendum campaign you would have been hard-pushed to find any mention whatsoever of these organisations anywhere in the media. In fact, you would have to have done a bit of research on Google to find out that these organisations were involved, who they are and why they were campaigning for independence.

A reasonable excuse for not including the views of these organisations is that nobody, other than those actually involved in the groups, would be interested. Of course, that might well not be the case and it is true that the membership of Women for Independence, for example, has increased since the referendum. Let us, however, assume, for the sake of argument, that this excuse holds true. How, then, do we explain the platform given to supporters of maintaining the Union that were outside the official Better Together campaign?

The Orange Order was held at arm's length by Better Together, who obviously wanted to avoid being embroiled in any sectarian feud. This, however, did not stop our media, both written and broadcast, from reporting at length about the 'Proud to be British' Orange rally in Edinburgh on September 12th 2014. Many at this rally were from England, Northern Ireland or even further afield so it was hardly a march by a Scottish organisation. The only ones interested in this rally would be those supportive of the Orange Order and those vehemently opposed to it. Which begs the question: why was this peripheral organisation given so much coverage? Furthermore, it was not reported as any kind of side-show but as an integral part of the referendum debate.

Again, however, it could be argued that the SNP was determined to dominate proceedings, while Better Together was more generous in allowing organisations that were not part of the mainstream campaign to have their moment in the limelight. Both scenarios, though, depend on the media being under the tight control of either side. It does not matter in this analysis whether the media was acting autonomously or under the control of Better Together; the editorials in all the papers made it plain which side they were supporting, and it was not the independence campaign.

Television and radio companies, meanwhile, protested constantly that they were impartial whenever accused of bias by the independence campaigners. Whether they were impartial or not is irrelevant here; of more importance is the fact that they were not under the control of the SNP. The side-lining of the other organisations involved in the YES campaign, therefore, was not the doing of Alex Salmond or his party.

Another pointer to this agenda is in the people the media chose not to include and one person in particular: Tommy Sheridan, who can hardly be described as a shrinking violet. Love him or loathe him; it is difficult to ignore him. Our media, however, went out of their way to do so. Whether you believe he does it to further his causes or out of egotistical self-interest, one thing is certain: Sheridan likes to be the centre of attention. During the referendum campaign the media pointedly refused to let Sheridan have his moment in the spotlight. Obviously they did not want the emphasis shifted away from Alex Salmond and the SNP.

Dr. John Robertson, of the University of the West of Scotland, along with colleagues, looked into the way the referendum was handled on television. They carried out this research from September 2012 until September 2013. The results were published at the start of 2014. Their findings showed, among other things, that the television news tended to focus on Alex Salmond and the SNP, rather than the independence campaign as a whole.

The research showed that 'the repeated association of the Yes/pro-independence campaign with the personal desires of Alex Salmond was regular and frequent. No such equation between No/anti-independence figures' personal drives and the No campaign was made.'[2]

BBC Scotland's answer to this was as follows:

Independence is the stated aim of the Scottish Government, of which Alex Salmond, as First Minister, is the head. He is, as such, a recognised voice for the independence argument and he has publicly stated his personal and political belief in independence.[3]

The BBC and STV both vehemently refuted Dr. Robertson's findings; BBC Scotland demanding to see his raw data. It is interesting to note, however, that neither television company has offered any data of its own. In fact, when questioned in Holyrood about the issue, both John Boothman, BBC Scotland Head of news and current affairs, and Ken McQuarrie, BBC Scotland Director, admitted that complaints about BBC coverage had increased since the start of the referendum campaign; neither of them, however, was able to provide MSPs with a breakdown of what the complaints were about.[4] So much for needing raw data!

Dr. Robertson's assertion that more time was spent on anti-independence statements than those in favour of independence was answered by BBC Scotland in a very candid and revealing manner. 'No one such figure (i.e. a recognised voice) is as easily identifiable for the anti-independence argument, given that three main political parties are involved, each with its own political agenda.'[5]

This, of course, is a rather specious argument; by the terms of its own argument, the BBC should have been allowing the other parties involved on the YES side a say as well. Any waffling excuses about 'main parties' etc. would be complete nonsense on two counts: this was not a general election, nor was it a UK-wide vote. Essentially, this was a frank admission that BBC Scotland was solely identifying the SNP with the campaign for independence.

Such a tactic, however, is fraught with danger; what would happen if everyone actually liked Alex Salmond? Walkers would be the first to admit that their association with Gary Lineker and his 'Mr. Nice Guy' image has been a major factor in their dominance of the crisp market in Britain. It was perfectly possible that the same thing could happen with Alex Salmond; everyone might end up rushing to vote for Scottish independence due to its identification with him.

Companies have discovered, however, that it is possible

for their products to get a negative connotation from their association with certain personalities. Churchill Insurance, for example, had to get rid of Martin Clunes from its adverts when he was disqualified from driving for six months. There are even worse associations than that; who would buy a Stylophone these days given its identification with a certain shamed celebrity? And Heinz must give thanks every day that having Gary Glitter as the face of its tomato soup went no further than one commercial!

Obviously, Salmond is hardly in the same league as Gary Glitter or Rolf Harris and any newspaper, television company or even blogger that implied that he was would soon find themselves in court. The best way to conjure up a negative image of Alex Salmond was to make it appear that he was the one that was hogging the limelight, of his own volition.

This kind of thing becomes self-fulfilling; the more the media pushed Alex Salmond into our consciousness the more we would believe that he wanted it that way. They could now report that the whole referendum was just about Salmond's ego; without mentioning, of course, that they were the ones that had made it that way!

One last word on this topic by Dr. Robertson is worth noting. The identification of the independence campaign with Alex Salmond on television was marked whenever a new story was being introduced; especially in the opening segment of the news programme when the upcoming stories would be announced. If there was bad news for the YES campaigners, this tended to be announced along the lines of 'Alex Salmond under pressure!'[6] Such headlines will also be familiar to those that get their news in the papers.

Fresh poll blow for Salmond as six in 10 Scottish voters now reject independence amid growing fears over the pound.[7]

Independence referendum: Blow for Alex Salmond as Record poll reveals Yes campaign support has stalled.[8]

B&Q boss's hammer blow for Alex Salmond.[9]

Alex Salmond's independence bandwagon stalls on his "Black Wednesday"[10]

Setback for Salmond as Chinese back a "strong, prosperous, united UK"[11]

These are just a few of the many headlines that can be found with a simple Google search. The whole media, then, mounted their own version of the campaign, bringing Alex Salmond to the front and associating him in the minds of their readers, listeners and viewers as the face of independence. Other campaigners for independence were effectively airbrushed out, making the whole focus on one man.

The clever part of this media campaign was to make us believe that this focus on Alex Salmond was all the doing of the man himself. We were being led into a belief that Alex Salmond was a power-crazed megalomaniac and the whole referendum was just an extension of his insane ego.

In December 2009, at a meeting of the audit committee at Holyrood, Lord George Foulkes, Labour MSP for Lothians, called Alex Salmond, 'Il Duce'. When challenged, he claimed it was a 'slip of the tongue' but referred to Salmond's supposed need to be 'minister for everything'.[12]

It was rather a strange phrase to come up with as a 'slip of the tongue'; usually such claims are made when somebody swears or gets a name wrong. A prime example was James Naughtie introducing Culture Secretary, Jeremy Hunt, as 'Jeremy Cunt'. That is a classic case of what is known as a 'Freudian Slip'. Calling someone 'Il Duce' hardly fits into this category.

The truth is that politicians are not renowned for thinking on their feet. Witness them being interviewed on television and they will rarely answer a question directly; preferring to stick doggedly to their pre-written arguments.

The great quotes that we read from politicians are usually well thought-out or written by someone else. Even Julius Caesar, who left many memorable sayings to posterity, could only resort to emptying a bucket of shit over an opponent's head during a heated debate in the Forum. Foulkes's 'slip of the tongue', therefore, was anything but.

There is a wide array of infamous dictators to choose from and Foulkes probably had his 'Il Duce' remark prepared well in advance. There is no denying the fact that Alex Salmond is not slim; the 'Il Duce' slur, then, was perfectly calculated to portray him as the modern equivalent of the fat, swaggering, Italian dictator. The knee-jerk comparison when claiming that someone is a dictator is to say that they are like Hitler. This, however, shows a distinct lack of imagination and has become something of a cliché; but, politicians being what they are, it has not stopped some of them from indulging in this particular simile.

Getting in early was Anne Moffat, Labour M.P. for East Lothian, who said, in 2007, 'Proportional representation gave Germany Adolf Hitler and in Scotland to a lesser degree we've had the member for Banff and Buchan.'[13] She claimed, of course, that she was referring to the voting system, rather than Alex Salmond; so why mention him?

Tom Harris, Labour's media adviser and M.P. for Glasgow South, made one of those 'Downfall' videos for his blog at the start of 2012.[14] Everyone must be familiar by now with this video, which shows Hitler ranting and raving at his generals. A quick search on YouTube will show all the different ways this clip has been used, with people adding their own subtitles to spoof their personal bête noire. Harris was not the first to lampoon somebody with this video, and he certainly was not the last, so it might seem churlish to condemn him for it. It came, however, in the midst of a lot of bile being flung in Salmond's direction and was just one more attempt to portray him as a blustering bully of a dictator.

Later that year, the historian David Starkey joined in by reportedly saying, 'Alex Salmond is a democratic Caledonian Hitler, although some would say Hitler was more democratically elected.'[15] He went on to point out that Salmond was demonising the English in the same way that Hitler had demonised the Jews.

Starkey is one of those people from a working-class background that feels he needs to act snootier than the upper-class folk he now mixes with. His cringe-worthy over-enunciation of words, for example, saying 'parl-y-a-ment' instead of saying the word the same way as everyone else, as well as his forelock-tugging devotion to the history of kings and queens, is testament to his desire to detach himself from his roots.

He also likes to court controversy; in many ways emulating the historical royal characters he loves so much. He blamed the riots that took place in England in 2011 on white youths being influenced by black culture and called Scotland, Ireland and Wales 'feeble little countries'. He has also hurled insults in the direction of, among others, David Cameron, Gordon Brown and Boris Johnson. He even compared the Queen to Goebbels![16]

His attack on Salmond, therefore, could be seen in the context of just one more verbal assault by a man that seems to enjoy lashing out at everybody. Coming, as it did, among a plethora of similar attacks against Salmond, it was one more justification for those attacks to take place.

In January 2012, Jeremy Paxman was unequivocal when he interviewed Alex Salmond on Newsnight. He said, 'I'm comparing you to Mugabe. Implicit in that is the idea that this is a one-party state. Implicit in that assumption is that there is only one party that can rule Scotland.'[17] Paxman was not the first to raise the spectre of Robert Mugabe; Lord Cormack made the same comparison a couple of months earlier in the House of Lords, throwing a comparison to Ian Smith into the mix for good measure.[18]

The comparisons to despots kept coming so that, as well

as those outlined above, by February 2012 Alex Salmond had already been compared to Kim Jong-Il, Genghis Khan, Nicolae Ceausescu, Nero, and Slobodan Milosevic.[19] It was getting so bad that the website Wings Over Scotland started up a game of 'Alex Salmond Dictator-Comparison Bingo!'[20]

Of course, most of these references were kept oblique; meaning that whoever uttered them could claim that they were merely emphasising a particular point. For example, Lord Forsyth's Kim Jong-Il comparison was to do with sixteen and seventeen-year-olds being allowed to vote in the referendum. His witty remark was, 'Only nine countries in the world give 16 and 17-year-olds the vote. They include North Korea and Cuba, which also have leaders with a high opinion of themselves.'[21] Cue an outbreak of laughter among those of the noble lords and ladies that were still awake.

Among the places allowing under-eighteens the vote, and which Lord Forsyth studiously avoided mentioning, are Austria, certain parts of Germany, the Isle of Man and Jersey. These are hardly what you would call Communist dictatorships; Jersey, especially, is as keen a worshipper at the altar of Mammon as you will find anywhere in the world. So, yet again, why mention North Korea and Cuba at all?

Strangely, Forsyth and the rest were, wittingly or unwittingly, following the advice of one of those to whom they were comparing Alex Salmond; one Adolf Hitler. Hitler said, in his polemical work Mein Kampf, about propaganda that its 'chief function is to convince the masses, whose slowness of understanding needs to be given time in order that they may absorb information; and only constant repetition will finally succeed in imprinting an idea on the memory of the crowd.' In other words, if you repeat a lie often enough and for long enough people will come to accept it as the truth.

So the population of Scotland, and of the UK in general,

was drip-fed the idea that Salmond was a dangerous man; a potential dictator and despot. This idea was reinforced by the media every time Salmond or his party complained about some item on television or in the newspapers. The media could show as much bias as they liked; if Salmond complained then he was obviously being dictatorial about what the media could and could not say.

Of course, there has to be some basis for such propaganda; for example, Hitler pointing to Jewish bankers and financiers, whom people in poverty were only too willing to accept as a convenient scapegoat. Those in favour of keeping the Union looked for some reason for their assertions that Salmond was a power-hungry dictator. They found, not a reason, but a rationalisation; and a specious one at that.

The so-called reason for comparing Salmond with all these dictators was that he ruled the SNP with an iron fist; policy was not made collectively, but by the leader. 'The leader decides and others follow,' one Scottish Labour spokesperson said.[22] Others spoke of Salmond and an 'inner circle' running the party and making policy.[23] Jim Sillars, former Deputy Leader of the SNP, joined in, saying,

Today, the SNP is the most leadership controlled party in the UK. If I did not know better, I would easily believe the leaders had been schooled in the old communist party, where the top, the elite, made the decisions and the rest fell into step automatically, with not a word of dissent.[24]

The bile from Sillars can be explained by his bitterness at never being party leader himself; while the assertions by a Labour Party member and the Daily Mail were obviously politically motivated. Such statements, however, seeped into the public consciousness; especially when bloggers helped to broadcast the message that Salmond was in total control of his party and was seeking to have the same control over Scotland.

It is rather strange that Labour and Conservative chose this tactic, since they were both instrumental in bringing American presidential-style elections to the fore. In the 1980s the Conservative Party and the Conservative press concentrated on the failings of the leader of the Labour Party during election campaigns. Michael Foot was portrayed as a senile, bumbling, old fool, who believed in socialist principles and Keynesian economic theories that were old-fashioned and out of step with the modern world.

In contrast, Margaret Thatcher was seen as a go-getting, energetic powerhouse, who was going to make everyone in the country rich and stand up to 'Johnny Foreigner'. Britain was going to be 'Great' again. Keynes, Beveridge, consensus, planned economies and trades unions were to be swept aside as hangovers from the past. Great pains were taken to portray Thatcher as the one to lead us all to the Promised Land. For example, you never, ever saw a photograph or a video clip of her relaxing; she was always doing something, whether it be reading documents or speaking to others. She was the new face of Britain; always busy, always making money. She even had elocution lessons to make her sound better.

Neil Kinnock was another that was portrayed as a bungling buffoon; another Labour man that was linked to the past. Even his lack of support for the striking miners did not count in his favour as far as the media were concerned; it only served to make him look more cowardly. Up against John Major, Thatcher's successor, whose own people had a hard time portraying him as anything other than boring, Kinnock felt the full force of the scathing Conservative press. Who can forget that 1992 headline in the Sun that asked the 'last person to leave Britain' to 'please turn out the lights'?[25]

Labour bumbled about for a while yet before coming up with Tony Blair; a man that looked like a Tory, spoke like a Tory, came from the same background as most Tories and claimed to be an admirer of Thatcher. Blair swept to power in 1997 and the cult of the leader was complete. Look at the leaders of the three main parties nowadays; hardly a grey hair between them. Everything is focused on the party leader, who has to tick all the boxes on looks, presentation, voice timbre, clothes and even marital partner. U.K. politics has become, to quote W.B. Yeats, 'no country for old men'.

In such an environment it was, perhaps, inevitable that the Unionist campaign would focus almost exclusively on Alex Salmond. The accusations about him being a despot and totalitarian, however, were completely disingenuous considering how much the UK parties rely on a certain kind of leader to get them elected. This reliance gives the leader a great deal of say over the direction and policies of the party, making said leaders just as despotic and totalitarian as they claimed Salmond was.

One more rationalisation for these portrayals of Alex Salmond came through during the referendum campaign. He was accused of cynicism and opportunism in changes to his own, and his party's policies; surely this showed how power-crazed he was?

Every political party has to make compromises in order to get elected. In the 1980s many Tories were in favour of privatising everything and Thatcher's claim that there was no such thing as society was no throwaway remark. To most Thatcherites the Welfare State was anathema; to their minds everyone should keep what they earn and not have to pay taxes to support those that cannot or, as the Tories see it, will not, look after themselves. Knowing that most people in Britain, and even many in their own party, did not share their extremist views, they had to compromise and only go as far as society allowed them.

Equally, the Labour Party had to compromise many of its principles in order to get elected. The huge lurch to the Right under Blair would have dismayed even Roy Jenkins, Shirley Williams and the rest, while those that had introduced the Welfare State after WWII would have barely recognised their party. New Labour, as it called itself, even got Rupert Murdoch on board; it must have sickened Neil Kinnock to see The Sun call on its readers to vote Labour!

And then we have the Liberal Democrats, who made a deal with the devil and got into bed with the Tories for the price of a referendum on an alternative voting system. It was the biggest betrayal of Liberal principles since Joseph Chamberlain crossed the floor of the House. Even Lloyd George's coalition came nowhere close; at least he was in control and was able to pass many Liberal measures. The only way Nick Clegg followed Lloyd George was in getting embroiled in a 'cash for honours' scandal.[26]

It was obviously disingenuous of the U.K. parties to accuse Alex Salmond of opportunism; they had all let principle fall by the wayside in return for even a modicum of power. It was also hypocritical in the extreme.

Since its inception, there has really only been one main policy of the SNP: Scottish independence. No matter what policies the party might espouse for election to the Scottish or Westminster Parliaments, or which way it might vote in these institutions, Scottish independence is its be-all and end-all; in fact it is its whole raison d'être.

Much is made of the fact that, in the 1970s and 1980s, Alex Salmond was a republican, who wanted to abolish the monarchy altogether.[27] And yet, here he was, in the referendum campaign, advocating the retention of the monarchy in an independent Scotland. This was paraded as a sign that he could not be trusted. The only answer to this allegation is a question: so what?

It is just possible that many in Salmond's 'faction' realised that republicanism was not a vote winner. Are they not allowed to change their policy if they feel that the electorate is not amenable to such a huge step? After all, the first priority has always been an independent Scotland. Once that has been achieved then it is perfectly feasible, at some future date, for those wanting rid of the monarchy to campaign for election on a republican ticket. The SNP would probably no longer exist as a party, its goal having been reached; it would probably splinter into its different, constituent parts.

Despite the hypocrisy of the attacks on Salmond, they continued right up to the end of the campaign. Supporters of the Better Together side took to calling Alex Salmond 'Fishy'; this was especially true on Unionist blogs. It is a very obvious pun, but no less clever and effective for it. It summed up all the accusations and invective directed at Salmond in one, succinct word and reinforced the idea that he was somebody that was not to be trusted.

Even after the referendum was done and dusted some folk just could not help themselves. Alex Salmond was still incensed over the perceived bias of the BBC and said so in an interview with the Daily Record. A few days later Sir Christopher Bland, a former chairman of the BBC board of governors, called on the BBC to defend itself. He said that somebody ought to be 'saying "really, Salmond, you're a paranoid loser and you really shouldn't insult the BBC like that"'.[28] Well, not unless he ended up in charge of BBC funding at Westminster!

When it came to name-calling, however, it seemed that only one side was allowed to conjure up images of fascist dictators. In a breath-taking display of hypocritical effrontery, the Unionist press was outraged when Jim Murphy, a Labour member of Better Together, was called 'Quisling'. One newspaper said, 'for anyone, politician or not, to be called a Quisling because of their honestly-held beliefs in this referendum is an affront to democracy.'[29] Apparently, though, it was the pinnacle of the democratic process to call Alex Salmond 'Hitler' etcetera! Besides, Murphy was probably called 'Quisling', not because he was perceived as a traitor to Scotland, but because he was sharing a platform with the Tories.

All this negative propaganda directed at Alex Salmond was effective but more was needed to reinforce the idea that he was a dictatorial despot. What better way than to convince everyone that the SNP had always been a fascist party, full of Nazi sympathizers and slavish adherents to the leadership principle?

2

Ersatz Natz?

In October 2012 the renowned author, CJ Sansom, took a break from his novels set during the reign of Henry VIII. His latest work was an alternative history, called Dominion, which was set in a world where Churchill did not become Prime Minister in 1940 and Britain subsequently made peace with Germany and essentially became a vassal state. This sort of thing was not new, most notably being done before by Len Deighton.

Ransom is a very popular author, as can be seen from his sales, and his large fanbase always eagerly awaits the release of his next novel. If reviews on Amazon are anything to go by, however, his fans were not too enamoured with this departure from his usual work. The family of Enoch Powell was none too happy either!

It is a huge leap to make to go from Powell's 'Rivers of Blood' speech to him being a Nazi sympathiser. Powell was, like Churchill, overwhelmingly British and deeply proud of the British Empire. Also like Churchill, he had been advocating war with Germany for years and even went so far as to call Chamberlain and Halifax 'traitors' for their appeasement of Hitler.[1] As soon as war was declared he rushed back from Australia to enlist. These actions hardly sound like those of someone that would consent to being in bed with the Nazis!

Sansom is well-known for his methodical research and attention to detail in his Tudor novels; he is, after all, a PhD in History. It appeared, however, that, although Sansom might be an expert on Fifteenth and Sixteenth-Century England, he had no great understanding of modern history. This was demonstrated most clearly in the way that the Scottish National Party was portrayed in his book. It is beyond the realms of credibility that the SNP would have been willing to collaborate with a Nazi government in the UK. Putting aside all idealistic considerations, the whole raison d'être of the SNP was to be free of Westminster, whether it be Nazi, Communist, Tory, Labour or any other kind of political persuasion. Obviously Sansom did not understand that.

He took this theme further at the end of his novel, where he explained the reasoning behind his alternative history. Much of this explanation was merely a diatribe against the SNP, which he claimed was 'deeply dangerous' and 'with no politics in the conventional sense, believing only in the old dream that the unleashing of 'national spirit' and 'national pride' can solve a country's problems.'[2]

This misrepresentation of what the SNP is all about was to become a major theme of the referendum campaign. Not only were things skewed to make it look as if a YES vote was a vote for the SNP but it was also being touted as a vote for Fascism. This was, of course, ridiculous and would have been hard to maintain as a serious strategy. Another book, however, arrived in 2013 to bolster this argument and give it a veneer of credibility and respectability.

'Fascist Scotland' was written by Gavin Bowd, a lecturer in French at St. Andrews University. In the book he details where in Scotland Fascism gained adherents and the general sympathy for Fascism and Nazism among the Scottish aristocracy. He also writes about how Mosley failed to gain many followers in Scotland because he was not bigoted enough; he did not discriminate against Catholics or the Irish.

One chapter in his book, however, is what everyone seemed to concentrate on. In this chapter he talks of the SNP and the attraction of Fascism to some of its leading members. It was hardly surprising that most attention is focused on this part of the book; the author himself speaks of it as if it is the whole point of the work.[3]

The fact is that in the 1920s and 1930s most people had a flirtation with Fascism, Communism or both. Fascism appealed to many in the Fabian Society and the Labour Party in general, as well as to Liberals and Conservatives. This seems to be pretty much accepted by, and acceptable to, everyone. No big deal is made of it; the people involved made a mistake and moved on.

If anyone wanted to go digging around in this period of history they could find all manner of embarrassing facts that could be thrown at today's political parties. For example, the Fabians were great believers in eugenics as a way of making things better for the working classes. And before any Tories start sniggering, Arthur Balfour was a leading member of the Eugenics Society, as was William Beveridge from the Liberals. Eugenics, nowadays, is considered to be part-and-parcel of Nazi ideology; should we therefore condemn our three main political parties for previously harbouring proto-Nazis in their midst?

Bowd, however, has an ace up his sleeve; MI5 investigated members of the SNP during the Second World War. That should be enough to convince anyone that the SNP is a special case; but, in reality, it is not as cut-and-dried as all that.

Our intelligence services do not have a great track record, it must be said. They were riddled with Communist spies from top to bottom and concentrated all their efforts on investigating Trades Union leaders when they would have done better to look into the students at Cambridge University. But, then, most of them came from there themselves and they were an integral part of the Establishment.

Speaking of the Establishment; that is where all the real spies were lurking. There was Lord Sempill, a relative of the Royal Family, who passed military secrets to the Japanese. Incredibly, this character was allowed to simply retire and live the rest of his life unmolested. Mosley himself was linked to the Royal Family. He was interned from 1940 to 1943 and then pretty much left alone. And then there was the Duke of Windsor, who had to be moved to the Caribbean because of his links to Nazi Germany.

After the war we had the Burgess, McLean, Philby and Blunt spy ring. The first three ran off to Russia while Blunt, like others before him, was left to live a privileged life in peace. There are still rumours that a fifth man was involved. No doubt our intelligence services knew full well who he was and covered it all up as usual.

So anyone that was investigated by MI5 was in pretty high-ranking company. And, given the track record of our intelligence and security services, it is hardly a damning indictment to have been under such investigation. That has not, however, stopped folk claiming that the SNP was a Fascist organisation.

More ammunition was forthcoming in early 2014 with the publication of a book that had nothing whatsoever to do with Scotland, the SNP or Fascism for that matter. 'Danubia' was a part-travelogue, part history, by the writer Simon Winder. In it he waxed lyrical about the Habsburgs and their empire, while telling his readers about the places he visited throughout the old Austro-Hungarian dominions.

The Habsburgs were the epitome of the greedy, self-serving families of the Middle Ages. Through a series of arranged marriages they spread their influence throughout Europe, and even to America under the Spanish branch of the family. Once ensconced, however, they kept things in the family by only marrying cousins, etcetera. Such a restricted gene pool obviously led to trouble and the family was notorious for producing offspring that were insane or feeble-minded. It also led to the grotesque facial deformity known as the Habsburg Jaw, which made some of them look like the monstrous offspring of an unnatural union between Bruce Forsyth and Jimmy Hill. This affliction meant that many of the family had problems with eating and even speaking properly.

To Simon Winder, however, the Habsburgs, especially the ones ruling Austria and the East, presided over a benevolent, peaceful and multi-cultural paradise. Everyone apparently lived together in harmony. He seems to ignore completely the long fight that the Magyars had to gain equality in their own country and the Protestant church of Transylvania, the most tolerant church in Europe, which was destroyed under the Habsburgs. In fact, anyone that was a Protestant in the Habsburg dominions was persecuted; a prime example was in the Spanish Netherlands, from which Protestant Holland managed to break away.

Winder warmed to his theme in an article for Standpoint magazine.[4] He said, 'The lesson of the Habsburg Empire's demise is probably that multinational states are extremely valuable.' Really? It obviously does not occur to him that such states are often the cause of the problems in the first place. Britain's dumping of a cache of Protestants into the north of Catholic Ireland is an obvious case in point, while most of the ethnic troubles in Africa stem from European 'divide and rule' colonial policies.

After telling us how Franz Ferdinand was planning all manner of federation schemes before his assassination, Winder goes on, 'Before the catastrophe of the First World War very few of the Empire's inhabitants imagined that independence was even a rational option.'[5]

Winder mentions the assassination of Franz Ferdinand, so he is obviously aware of it. He seems blissfully unaware, however, of the reasons behind it. The assassination had been meticulously planned but ended in abject failure. Through sheer luck one of the conspirators, Gavrilo Princip, managed to shoot the Archduke and his wife. At his trial Princip had this to say, 'I am a Yugoslav nationalist, aiming for the unification of all Yugoslavs, and

I do not care what form of state, but it must be freed from Austria.'[6] So much for that big, happy family that was the Habsburg Empire!

Through the centuries the Balkans has had a hell of a time of it; the Macedonians, the Romans, the Ottomans and the Habsburgs all had their empires stretching into it. And then they had the Soviet Union. But, according to Winder, they were better off under the yoke of imperialism than they are now. Perhaps the whole world should take heed and Canada, Australia, New Zealand, the U.S.A, Ireland and half of Africa should all vote to come back to the British Empire! Or what about all those Latin American nations; surely they would be better off being ruled by Spain and Portugal?

Winder shows remarkable naivety in his praise for the Habsburg Empire and multi-national states in general. In the Nineteenth Century such states were considered corrupt and inefficient. The Ottoman Empire was the epitome of such a state; even conservative UK politicians, who wanted it maintained as a buffer to Russian ambitions, viewed it in this way. Liberals, on the other hand, cheered at every reversal of fortune suffered by the Ottoman Empire and supported the national aspirations of Greece and other Balkan nations.

Nationalism was seen as a liberal political philosophy in the Nineteenth Century; it is only in the second half of the Twentieth Century that it has gained a negative reputation. Liberals nowadays will throw up their hands in horror at the mere mention of nationalism, forgetting that their liberal forebears, a hundred years ago, espoused it with enthusiasm.

In our modern, liberal democracies every effort is made to avoid the dreaded term nationalism. This puts pressure on those to the Right of the mainstream political spectrum as they have to steer a careful course between patriotism and nationalism. Certainly there are those on the lunatic fringes, who like to march around in bedsheets or in Nazi attire proclaiming their nationalist credentials. In the main, however, patriotism and nationalism are declared to be separate entities; even though there is often not much to choose between them.

And so we get the ridiculous situation where what is called patriotism when we do it is called nationalism when a foreign nation does the same. Take 'Armed Forces Day,' for example, when the UK celebrates its army, navy and air force with marches, demonstrations and fly-pasts. Such a show in Russia would be called nationalistic, whereas in Britain it is merely patriotic. We are all made to feel frightened when North Korea parades its military might; when we do it, however, there is nothing remotely provocative about it. These double standards were evident during the referendum campaign.

UKIP has become a major force in England, stealing voters from the Conservatives in Tory heartlands. In response to this threat, David Cameron had a reshuffle in July 2014, in which he promoted Eurosceptics, such as Philip Hammond, the new Foreign Secretary, to the cabinet.[7] The Government has also made noises about withdrawing from the European Convention on Human Rights. It looks increasingly like the political zeitgeist in England is heading in the direction of pulling out of Europe. Is this nationalism or is it patriotism?

The major concern of those calling for a withdrawal from the European Union is its policy on the free movement of labour. The spectre of hordes of Eastern Europeans swarming into the UK to take up jobs and housing and place a massive burden on the NHS is being cast before us more and more these days. Immigration is being blamed for everything wrong in Britain, including robbery, violent crime and even child abuse. The more we go into it, the more nationalistic England is looking!

Muslims too have come under the scrutiny of English nationalists. There are stories about plans to force Sharia Law upon councils. Anybody that goes into a mosque is a potential terrorist, out for British blood. And while there still seems to be a massive cover-up of members of the Establishment being involved in child abuse, much is made of Pakistani men being in a paedophile ring. Inductive logic is used to try to convince us all that child abuse is part-and-parcel of Islam; they would all be at it, given half a chance! This latter element has echoes of the old 'Blood Libel' scare stories about the Jews.

All of this was swept under the carpet while the referendum on Scottish independence was taking place. In fact, the mainstream UK parties made it plain that the BNP, UKIP, the EDL, and the SDL had nothing to do with the official Better Together campaign. This had important implications when it came to accusing YES supporters of abuse and intimidation; it also left Better Together free to argue that the SNP was no better than the Nazis.

Perhaps the most blatant example of this argument was Alistair Darling's infamous 'Blood and Soil Nationalists' slur. He has denied vociferously that he said it and the New Statesman helped fudge the issue by claiming that they had misquoted him. The offending phrase was replaced by '...inaudible mumble.' Well, that certainly helped to clear things up! The 'corrected' interview, however, still reflects badly on Darling.

NS: Salmond has successfully redefined the SNP as [representing] a civic nationalism . . .

Darling: Which it isn't . . .

NS: But that's what he says it is. Why do you say it isn't? What is it? Blood and soil nationalism?

Darling: At heart . . . [inaudible mumble] If you ask any nationalist, 'Are there any circumstances in which you would not vote to be independent?' they would say the answer has got to be no. It is about how people define themselves through their national identity.'[8]

Now, that sounds pretty conclusive. Darling denies point-blank that the SNP is promoting 'civic nationalism'; so what does he think that it is? He says nothing against the 'Blood and soil' assertion; in fact, he speaks of people defining themselves 'through their national identity'. That certainly sounds as if he agrees with the accusation.

Stuart Campbell, on his website, Wings Over Scotland, did an excellent article on this, showing that, really, there are only two types of nationalism: civic or ethnic. The fact that Darling denies that the proposed independent Scotland comes under 'civic nationalism' automatically means that he considers it to be about 'Blood and soil'.[9]

The phrase 'Blood and Soil' is one that the Nazis used to describe their brand of nationalism: 'Blut und Boden'. It was all about racial purity; Germany for the Germans. It conjures up images of the Holocaust, the extermination of ethnic minorities; what is euphemistically called 'ethnic cleansing' these days. This is the type of nationalism that Alistair Darling and others were accusing the SNP of favouring and trying to hide this true nature from the electorate. It was a frightening idea.

Fundamental to any ethnic nationalism is the need for an enemy; of course, the perceived enemy of the SNP was obvious. Composer James MacMillan argued that there was a deep anti-English agenda in Scotland, which the SNP was exploiting and, indeed, fostering. He linked this to the anti-Irish bigotry that is still to be found throughout the country.[10] Strangely, he does not seem to realise that the very ones that promoted anti-Irish bigotry in Scotland were dead-set against Scottish independence. And his evidence for this anti-English sentiment appeared to be purely anecdotal and third-hand at that!

In January 2012, Johann Lamont said, 'What is my problem with David Cameron? He is a Tory. What is Alex Salmond's problem with him? He's English.'[11] Without a hint of irony, she went on, in the same article, to complain that Alex Salmond and the SNP were 'making arguments for us that we are not making'!

The press decided to go to town with this supposed hatred for the English. 'Savage racism turning Scotland into a no-go zone for the English,' screamed the Daily Mail. To illustrate this they told us the story of a couple being forced out of their home by pro-independence thugs and...er...that was it. The rest of the article was the usual stuff about 'cybernats' and the intimidation of NO campaigners; nothing at all about threats or violence toward English folk.[12]

The Telegraph joined in as well. 'Anti-English racists terrorising the No campaign in Scotland,' one of their headlines screamed. The article, however, had nothing to do with anti-English attacks; it was all about some lunatic fringe group, called Siol nan Gaidheal supposedly following Jim Murphy around.[13] So where does the anti-English element come in? Well, this group, whose name means 'Seed of the Gaels,' is all about opposing 'white settlers' and English imperialism. It was automatically being assumed that this lot were part of the official YES campaign, which, again, showed the hypocrisy of the Unionists. Remember, they had extremists on their side as well; and plenty of them. Nobody, however, was allowed to suggest that these extreme British nationalists were part-and-parcel of the NO campaign.

We even had John Major being wheeled out of whatever cupboard he has been stored in, calling the independence campaign anti-English. His evidence? Why, the referendum vote was being held not long after the Bannockburn commemorations![14] This was hardly what you could call adding to the debate.

The fact is that there was no anti-English rhetoric whatsoever from anyone connected with the independence side. That, of course, did not deter the media from constantly claiming that anti-Englishness was the whole basis of the campaign. This became a sort of mantra from Better Together and the media; the hope was that if they kept repeating the lie often enough then everyone would end up believing it.

Not one shred of proof was ever put forward for these claims. Reading in the Mail about the couple leaving their home due to intimidation, it was hard not to feel that we were not being told the whole story. There are always tales in the papers about neighbours falling out and one of them claiming that they were discriminated against. The fact that this particular story was not backed up with any evidence, or corroboration from witnesses was highly suspicious to say the least. And, in any case, even if it were true, it appeared to be an isolated incident; hardly evidence of a whole nation afire with racial hatred!

The truth was that it was difficult to substantiate claims that the SNP was anti-English; there was no evidence at all. Anecdotes do not really prove anything, other than that there are idiots out there that will pick on people just because they are different. There is plenty of such anecdotal evidence of attacks of an anti-Irish nature in Scotland, which nobody wants to know about; only hard statistics matter. Why, then, should we accept such evidence when it comes to attacks being anti-English?

With a serious lack of anti-English rhetoric coming from the SNP, Better Together and the media had to go to ridiculous lengths to rationalise their accusations.

'Both (George) Foulkes and Jill Stephenson, an emeritus professor of history at Edinburgh University, believe the SNP leader and his colleagues often speak in anti-English 'code'.

'Any time you hear senior members of the SNP complain about "Westminster", or "the Tories", or "London", what they are really talking about is the English. And supporters know it,' says Stephenson.'[15]

Such statements are, of course, risible, but at the same time pretty scary. These were people in positions of authority, who folk would assume would know what they were talking about.

The truth was that everyone resident in Scotland had a vote in the referendum, including the English. From the Hooray Henries and Henriettas of St. Andrews University to the guy from London cleaning the toilets at Central Station; all of them had a say in Scotland's future. Why would the SNP attempt to alienate these voters by telling them that they are not wanted?

A major pointer to the kind of nationalism the SNP was advocating is the fact that expat Scots did not have a vote in the referendum. There are none so patriotic as those that no longer live in their home country and there would have been many Scots living abroad, all misty-eyed about their 'Granny's Heilan' Hame' in Springburn, who would have jumped at the chance to vote for Scottish independence. That such people did not have a vote, while everybody that lived in Scotland did, is testament to the fact that the SNP were envisaging a civil nationalism.

Contrast this with the Tories extending the vote in general elections to Britons living and working abroad. At present this right expires after fifteen years; the Tories are now looking to make this a lifelong entitlement. These expats can vote for a candidate in the constituency in Britain where they were previously registered.[16] It makes a complete mockery of the First-Past-The-Post voting system, which is meant to ensure that MPs represent their constituents.

It also makes ridiculous Norman Tebbit's infamous 'Cricket Test'.[17] Tebbit and his Tory colleagues believed that immigrants should show their loyalty to their new home by supporting the England cricket team, rather than Pakistan, India or the West Indies. Presumably this 'loyalty' would extend to not voting in elections in their homeland but, instead, concentrating on being British citizens.

This is still a hot topic for Tories in this day and age. Look through any letters or comments section in the Telegraph, Times, Daily Mail or Sun and you will find numerous complaints about the lack of integration by immigrants. They say that immigrants should have to prove to everyone that they are now loyal to Britain or they should be thrown out. Meanwhile, British emigrants to other countries are to be saved from 'going native' by keeping their attachment to their home nation. How chauvinistic is that?

The lack of complaints from Labour and the Liberal Democrats on this issue shows that they tacitly support it. It is hypocritical in the extreme that these parties have been accusing the SNP of ethnic nationalism while ignoring one of their Better Together partners indulging in it. In fact, the Labour Party itself has not been averse to advocating a bit of ethnic nationalism when it suits; Gordon Brown promised 'British jobs for British workers' in 2007.[18]

Mentioning Gordon Brown leads on to another item that was swept under the carpet: anti-Scottish bigotry. This is something that the media ignored altogether over the past few years. The anti-Scottish bile directed at Brown when he was Prime Minister would have resulted in prosecutions if he had been of another nationality.[19] It seems, however, that anti-Scottish rhetoric is perfectly acceptable.

It was not all that long ago that the Daily Record was in the forefront of complaints about the portrayal of Scottish people on television. If there was a drunk, a junkie, a violent psychopath or down-and-out needed in a television drama, the chances were that he, or she, would have a Scottish accent. It is a stereotype as bad as any stupid Irishman, Afro-Caribbean drug-dealing pimp, arrogant, martial German, forelock-tugging, happy-in-poverty Cockney or tight-fisted, money-worshipping Yorkshireman. This offensive stereotype still appears occasionally on our screens; the Daily Record, however, has become strangely silent about it.

The Scottish media is equally reticent about claims that Scotland is a nation of benefits junkies. It has been proven time and again that Scotland actually contributes more to the UK than it takes out. That, however, does not stop all the angry tirades from English folk that they are paying taxes so that Scottish people can get free prescriptions.[20] Previously our media would have been up in arms about such dangerous nonsense but it appeared that there was a moratorium on reporting on anything anti-Scottish during the referendum campaign. Only stories about anti-Englishness, whether real or imagined, were allowed.

Another, rather strange, phenomenon that manifested itself in England, and was used to great effect by Better Together, was the accusation that the SNP was going to turn English people into 'foreigners'. The fear engendered by this word exposed a deep-seated, chauvinistic xenophobia. Stuart Campbell again did an excellent article on this subject on his website.[21]

Campbell, with an astuteness eluding most of the rest of us, picked up on the way the word 'uncomfortable' was usually in the same sentence as 'foreigner'. Why were they so uncomfortable at their relatives, friends or even themselves being labeled foreigners? After all, as Campbell pointed out, we are 'all foreigners to someone'. It certainly said more about the prejudices of the ones making the accusations than it did about the SNP.

Fearful predictions were made of needing passports, armed borders and families being broken asunder. It seemed to have escaped everyone's notice that it is an easy matter to travel back and forth between Britain and Ireland. It has only been relatively recently that you have needed to show a passport on such a journey; even then it is about security, rather than borders as such. And there has never been any problem either about Irish people living in Britain and vice-versa. How many armed border checks are there between Northern Ireland and the Irish Republic?

To sum up, then, the SNP was being presented as a fascist party, with links to Nazism, which peddled hatred of the English in order to establish an ethnic-nationalist state and which was determined to turn all English people into 'foreigners'. If the SNP dared to answer in kind, they were accused of lowering the tone of the debate and of using vile

42

insults.

And so we come to the next tactic in the Better Together campaign. While accusations were hurled at the SNP in the name of so-called truth, any accusations or name-calling going in the other direction raised shrill complaints of intimidation. This was the final part of the campaign of smear waged by Better Together; trying to convince everyone that the SNP was going all-out to intimidate opponents and voters.

3

The Cybernats

Remember how, away back in the olden days of steam-powered telly, when somebody would come on spouting something with which you disagreed and which maybe even angered you, you would shout and swear at the TV and maybe even throw something at it? The smug face on the screen would continue undaunted; secure in the knowledge that it could not hear the tidal wave of abuse being hurled at it in living rooms across the country.

In this modern age there is no escape and that smug face will usually end up in the newspapers, covered in tears and bubbling about the terrible things that have been said to it on Twitter. Nobody bothers shouting at the telly anymore; they can reach for their laptop, tablet or even phone and let the offending personage know exactly what they think of him or her. Nowadays, if you are going to step into the limelight and offer an opinion you have to be prepared for a backlash from people that disagree with you.

Some timid souls refuse to have a Twitter account, just in case they do not like what people say about them. There are plenty of blogs and online newspaper forums, however, for folk to vent their fury. The targets of these splenetic digital missives are bound to read at least some of them; if they were not narcissistic then they would not be in the public eye in the first place!

Others absolutely wallow in it all, like that woman Katie Hopkins. She might be a figure of hate but, to her type of person, that is much more preferable than anonymity. Frankie Boyle is another that enjoys it, though for different reasons. He seems to revel in the cut-and-thrust of online debate and in being able to outdo anyone that offers him abuse.

And offer abuse they do. Going back to the days when we would all shout at the telly, it was rare for any of us to offer a reasonable, well-thought-out debate to the figure on the screen. Instead, we would hurl all manner of invective, calling into question the person's parentage, intellectual abilities and sexual proclivities. It was probably just as well that the TV signal did not go in both directions.

Communications technology might have changed but people have not. A good dose of abuse is often more effective than a reasoned argument; it certainly makes the one dishing it out feel better! It is also a lot easier than trying to write a masterpiece of the debating art when you only have 140 characters, including spaces, to play with!

Most celebrities, politicians and what have you simply shrug it off; they do not know the people sending abusive Tweets, so why should they care? It only gets really worrying if it is the same person stalking you relentlessly. Most folk accept it as a downside of the job, like bad reviews or unfavourable articles in the press.

Much of the abuse can be put down to idiots; it does not matter who you are you will get these abusive Tweets at some point or other. Judy Finnigan was targeted when she defended footballer and convicted rapist Ched Evans on television.[1] The leader of the Scottish Conservatives, Ruth Davidson, has been the victim of homophobic abuse since she came into the public eye.[2] Even harmless presenter of Strictly Come Dancing, Claudia Winkleman, received a host of nasty Tweets when her daughter ended up in hospital after her Halloween costume caught fire.[3]

For once Katie Hopkins got something right when she said:

The sort of people who threaten to chop your head off (on Twitter) are not lurking at the end of your lane with a machete. They are at home squeezing their spots and playing Minecraft and dressing up as Brenda from Blackpool when their mum goes out to work.[4]

Politicians are ideal candidates for such abuse, which they

will get no matter which party they are in. Elections increase the incidence of such online activity and the referendum on Scottish independence was no different. What was different, however, was the way in which the media responded to this abuse on Twitter. Instead of either ignoring it or condemning it all, they decided to only be outraged by the abuse coming from one side. In fact, they contrived to ignore any abuse whatsoever that came from supporters of Better Together.

The organisers of the Better Together campaign were in a rather enviable position. They had ready-made scapegoats in the shape of all those that were excluded from being part of the official campaign. The Orange Order, UKIP and the Scottish Defence League, among others, could easily be blamed for anything untoward happening; and yet they could all be relied upon to vote against independence no matter what accusations were thrown in their direction. Since it was assumed that any abuse targeted at YES supporters came from those sources then it was not worth reporting such abuse; there was no point bringing the lunatic fringe into the debate.

The campaign for independence, on the other hand, had no such luxury. There were no scapegoats available so any online abuse of NO supporters was reported as coming from within the YES campaign itself. Since the media refused to acknowledge that any other organisation except the SNP was involved in the campaign, that party and its members were blamed relentlessly. In fact, the media went out of their way to make out that this was actually a concerted campaign of abuse organised at the very top of the SNP.[5]

It was George Foulkes that first coined the term 'Cybernats'. Although it sounds like something out of Doctor Who, it was actually the term he used to describe what he envisioned as a concerted, online campaign by Scottish Nationalists against him. The word soon caught on and, throughout the referendum campaign, it was used by the media to drive home their invention of the organised, intimidatory tactics of the SNP.

Every day we read in the papers about the online abuse that supporters of the Union had to put up with. The 'cybernats' supposedly targeted JK Rowling, David Bowie and various other celebrities, politicians and business people that had come out in support of a NO vote. Of course, not one word was said about abuse coming from the Unionist side, even though there was plenty of it.

If Alex Salmond was on fire and I had a hose I would wrap it around his fat neck and choke the lying bastard.

A can't actually understand who would like that cow sturgeon and her wife salmond. Disgusting couple.

Alex Salmond is a fat ugly wanker.

If Scotland leaves the Union boycott their goods. No friends with traitors. Nuke the sweaty socks.

Scotland are shit anyway they've only got andy murray an hes a wanker fuck Scotland and fuck murray

These are just a few of the many collected on the BritNat Abuse Twitter page.[6] 'BritNat' was a term invented by Stuart Campbell in answer to the ubiquitous 'cybernat'. Of course, it never caught on; primarily because the media refused point-blank to countenance the fact that such abuse by supporters of the Union existed. All we read and heard about was 'Cybernats this' and 'Cybernats that'; and yet, the media acted with indignation when they were accused of bias!

And there were even worse examples than those above. Nicola Sturgeon received death threats on Twitter, a NO campaign Facebook page threatened that bullets would be fired into SNP leaders and there were even death threats against Alex Salmond's father.[7] Nothing was said about these threats in the newspapers or any other media.

At last, abuse was directed at a high-profile supporter of independence that the media could not ignore: Andy Murray. It was on the night before the actual vote was to take place that Murray made the announcement on Twitter that he favoured an independent Scotland. The story was in the papers next morning, along with an account of the abuse he received; tellingly, one or two papers decided to hold off reporting on it until the day after the vote.[8] The papers that did report it on 18th September, however, made sure to mention that Murray was only the latest in a long line of celebrities to suffer abuse. Just so we were clear, all the celebrities listed had been verbally abused by the 'cybernats'.[9]

Incredibly, there were those that criticised Murray, implying that the abuse was his own fault for making his announcement on Twitter.[10] Nobody ever made that claim against any of the NO supporters that were abused!

It was left to a columnist, in the Telegraph of all places, to point out the hypocrisy of all the one-sided condemnation. Needless to say, her article was published on the 19th September when it was too late to make any difference. She asked, 'With the Yes campaign having to address and own up to abusers tagging on the cause - and it's a fair cop, when called out such people should be exposed - where was the outcry when Unionists did the same?'[11]

To misquote a twee and mawkish old saying: Unionism meant never having to say you're sorry! No apology was ever forthcoming from the NO side; there was no need for any, since we were led to believe that they behaved impeccably. Meanwhile, Alex Salmond was castigated for deploring *all* online abuse; all the media wanted from him was an abject apology and an admission that his 'cybernats' were to blame for everything.[12]

As well as continually showing the independence campaign in a negative light, there was a more sinister aspect to all these allegations. In January 2014 Jim Murphy, a leading campaigner for the Labour contingent of Better Together, called for 'cybernats' to be banned from being in the audience of referendum debates. He admitted himself that many online messages were anonymous so it was going to be problematic finding out who they were. Perhaps he envisaged a blanket ban on independence supporters. Whatever the specifics it was obvious that he wanted to be able to pick and choose who was going to be in the audience at debates.[13]

This would not be the last time that Murphy, and others in the Better Together campaign, would come straight out and state that the independence supporters were intimidating people and not just in cyberspace. Apparently NO posters were being ripped down while supporters of the Union were verbally abused on the street; one man even had an egg thrown at him! The poor soul managed to take time out from being treated for shell shock (sorry!) to get a picture taken of his injured shirt for the Daily Mail.[14]

The Mail might scream in its headline that it was presenting 'Damning Evidence' but, in reality, it was nothing of the sort. A couple of pictures and a few second-hand anecdotes are hardly proof of a concerted, nationwide campaign of intimidation. The stories featured did not really conjure up a vision of people living in terror; nobody was hurt.

That certainly was not the case when we heard of the treatment of YES supporters. An eighty-year-old man was badly beaten when campaigning for independence on Edinburgh's Royal Mile,[15] a woman was kicked in the stomach by a pro-Union campaigner,[16] and some pro-independence campaigners were attacked with kicks and punches when handing out leaflets outside Tynecastle.[17] It looked like the NO side was indulging in some intimidation tactics of its own, refusing to limit itself to either mere words or eggs.

Dr. Brooke Magnanti, whose article in the Telegraph we have already encountered, spoke of 'tumbleweeds' in the newspapers when it came to criticism of Better Together.[18] The same tumbleweeds were apparent when it came to reporting on the violence of the pro-Union supporters. Any newspaper that did deign to tell us about it always made sure to mention the 'cybernats' and the supposed intimidation practised by the independence campaigners.

Amazingly, reports of such incidents prompted pro-Union supporters to claim that they were a result of 'cybernat' intimidation! Apparently, all the complaints of bias and unfairness from the SNP had made the newspapers feel that they had to try to balance things out. They were now reporting on 'isolated incidents' in an attempt to make the NO campaigners seem as bad as those on the YES side; even though everybody was aware that the independence side was mounting an organised campaign.[19]

George Foulkes went even further than that, saying:

I deplore any physical violence but I think you have to be very careful about making claims about who is responsible.
I would deplore it. But I suspect it may be being exaggerated and twisted to create counter balance to the attacks Jim Murphy has had to suffer.'[20]

In other words, it was a pack of lies; another example of the perfidy of the SNP.

If somebody was 'exaggerating and twisting' stories then they were obviously wasting their time; hardly anyone knew anything about them. Meanwhile, we were still being fed stories about intimidation by independence campaigners. Apparently it was getting so bad that there were calls from the pro-Union side for there to be extra security at polling stations on September 18th.

One of the things that NO campaigners claimed to find particularly intimidating was that independence supporters would constantly film everyone on video recorders. As one NO supporter said, 'It's deliberate intimidation, particularly the filming. It's the kind of thing animal-rights nutters have done for years.'[21]

And yet, in the same article we are told that 'Much of it (intimidation by YES campaigners) was captured on film now circulating on YouTube.' One wonders if those YES campaigners felt as intimidated about being filmed as those on the NO side claimed to be! It also begs the question of what the amateur film-makers among the independence campaign were doing with those many hours of footage they were supposed to have taken. Either they were planning a blockbuster movie or they were going to send clips into 'You've Been Framed'. (They pay for every clip broadcast, you know!)

On the subject of videos and cameras, there were plenty there on the day that Jim Murphy was hit with an egg in Kirkcaldy. Other politicians have been hit with eggs in the past; the most memorable being John Prescott. Everybody remembers the Prescott incident, especially since he immediately chinned the perpetrator. Many in the right-wing press claimed that Prescott overreacted, while the one that wielded the egg is still seen in some quarters as a hero.[22] This time round it was a different story entirely.

The way the media went on about Murphy being egged made it appear to be a crime akin to the Kennedy assassination. It started off with him being hit with an egg.[23] Then it was Murphy and a cancer patient being hit with eggs.[24] By the start of September the story was that the 'Indy thug' had deliberately, and with malice aforethought, bought a half-dozen best free-range from Tesco for the sole purpose of assaulting Mr. Murphy.[25] Before we knew where we were the papers were telling us that Murphy had been pelted with eggs, seemingly by a gang of independence campaigners.[26] The poor man even had to suspend his talking tour of Scottish towns because of this intimidation.[27] What was that George Foulkes was saying about exaggeration?

While Jim Murphy, the Labour Party, Better Together and everyone in the media was banging on about organised campaigns of intimidation by the YES campaigners, our old friend Stuart Campbell was on the case again. He had spotted that the spontaneous crowd of NO supporters that gathered round Murphy in every town was anything but. He provided photographic evidence that showed that the same people were appearing in the crowd listening to Murphy.[28] It looked as if Murphy had an organised mob turning up at towns all over Scotland. That sounds a bit familiar!

Of course, none of the media bothered to pick up on Campbell's story, even though it should have been front-page news. It was pretty obvious why they ignored it; they could hardly keep harping on about intimidatory gangs of 'Indy thugs' following Murphy around if they let everyone know he was taking his own rent-a-mob with him!

Murphy himself was extremely confrontational when standing on his Irn Bru crates, shouting even though he had a microphone in his hand. He was reluctant to answer questions put to him by supporters of independence, preferring instead to launch into tirades about the SNP while a mob clapped and cheered.[29] As journalist and broadcaster Derek Bateman argued, it was extremely hypocritical of Murphy to indulge in 'rabble rousing' and then complain when he actually succeeded in rousing a rabble![30] Bateman also put forward the opinion that the whole business, eggs and all, smacked of being a stunt.

This idea is not as crazy or as paranoid as it might sound; stranger things have happened in the world of politics. While they were continually accusing the independence supporters of conducting an organised campaign of intimidation, perhaps Better Together was doing a bit of organising of its own.

There is a long history in Britain of agents provocateurs and infiltrators worming their way into any organisation that the Establishment does not like. Join any party on the extreme left or right and chances are that the woman sitting next to you at the meeting, the one that seems more enthusiastic than anyone else, is either with the police or in the pay of MI5. These infiltrators are in unions, student associations, even charities; is it too much to believe that they did not get involved in the independence campaign?

Okay, so maybe imagining it as being like some kind of conspiracy-theory movie is taking things a bit far, but there was definitely something strange going on. Trouble seemed to be following Jim Murphy around the country and, yet, the only thing in common about every town was that his wee travelling circus was with him.

And then there was all the business with the posters. According to what we were told, the 'Indy thugs' were going round defacing, and even destroying, posters that pro-Union campaigners had put up.[31] There was never any evidence presented, however, to show that it was actually independence campaigners that were doing these things, let alone that the whole thing was organised in any way. It could just as easily have been NO campaigners that were vandalising the posters in order to blame it on the other side.

The papers also reported on the violence that was happening; of course, they only told of violence perpetrated by YES campaigners and supporters.[32] There were violent crimes committed by both sides, none of it organised or coordinated; that would come after the referendum. It is also quite possible that not all of the violence was directly connected to the referendum.

Their like their counterparts the ira using intimidation etc

When you have PRO IRA group openly welcome at the Edinburgh SSnp march last year its a clue SNP=Sinn Fein different names same aims[33]

Comments like these are all over the internet; on blogs, on Facebook pages, on Twitter and on newspaper forums. As usual, when you scratch the surface in Scotland, the canker of sectarian bigotry is not too far underneath. In the interests of fairness and impartiality I searched around for similar comments coming from those on the pro-independence side; I could find none. It would seem that this was a phenomenon solely to be seen or heard among the opponents of independence.

And this kind of reasoning was not just to be found among the lunatic fringe on the internet. Astoundingly, The Telegraph allowed an article, by one Ruth Dudley Edwards, in which it is alleged that sectarian bigotry in Scotland stemmed from Irish immigrants and that the Irish harbour a bitter hatred toward the English.[34] That will come as a surprise to all the English tourists that travel to Ireland every year!

The writer uses anti-Catholic rhetoric and describes Ireland as a backward, insular place, which had to be dragged, kicking and screaming into the modern world by the European Union. She also employs rather provocative terms; but only when talking about the supporters of independence. For example, when talking of potential trouble at the planned Orange march in Edinburgh, she worries in case 'some of their (the Orange Order's) less disciplined members fall out with nasty elements of the "Yes" campaign.' This leaves no room for doubt that any trouble would be caused by the 'nasty' pro-independence campaigners. The only hope for things to pass off peaceably is if the Orange marchers keep their 'discipline' in the face of this onslaught.

In one paragraph she uses a non-sequitur to equate a possible future renunciation of the monarchy in Scotland as being equivalent to the country having its own version of the IRA. This is obviously aimed at a certain type of person and expecting a particular type of reaction.

She appeals to the same people in her concluding paragraph, which contains the crux of her whole argument: Scottish independence might destabilise Northern Ireland. She says:

Loyalists are already worked up because they reckon restrictions on flying the Union Flag and on Orange parades are an attack on their identity and their culture.' In this vulnerable state they could easily fall prey to 'skillful Sinn Fein opportunists'.[35]

It was rare to find such sentiments expressed in a national newspaper, rather than on some online Ulster Unionist blog. It was designed to appeal directly to those in Scotland that had an affinity with Loyalists in Ulster. In essence, it was a call to arms in the same vein as a speech by Edward Carson in the years before the First World War.

Of course, the comments section beneath the online version of the article hardly had anything to say about Scotland. It was all about Ireland and the Irish, with a good few anti-Catholic and anti-Irish comments thrown in for good measure. The writer had obviously reached her audience and the two sides in the independence referendum had been successfully conflated with the bitter divide in Northern Ireland.

Of course, stirring up such hatred is bound to have consequences. There are those that can get so heated that they believe that they are perfectly justified in resorting to violence. It is more than possible that the incidences of violence we were told about in the media were as a result of this sectarian hatred, rather than being directly connected to the referendum campaign. And who was fomenting this hatred? Why, people on the NO campaign side. An organised campaign of intimidation, no less!

Such conclusions can easily be dismissed out of hand but there is plenty of readily-available evidence, especially online, of Scottish independence being equated with Irish Republicanism. In fact, there is far more evidence to support this conclusion than there is of a concerted campaign of intimidation being waged by the SNP.

This conflation of Unionism and bigotry reached its climax once the vote on independence had actually been cast. On the morning of September 19th I had a look round the internet at the gloating of the Unionists for something to write on my blog. I looked at the Facebook page of a member of the Orange Order, where numerous

Union flags, pictures of Orange walks and references to Ulster abounded. Among all the gloating of him and his friends, he included a comment that seemed to make no sense at the time. He had to be somewhere that evening and was sorry that he was going to miss out on all 'the fun' in Glasgow's George Square.

That night we all discovered what 'the fun' was. Independence campaigners had been based at George Square in the days running up to the vote and there had been a good-natured, carnival atmosphere; much to the disgust of the media, who pretty much ignored it. A party was planned in the Square for September 19th, win or lose, to celebrate the campaign and to thank everyone for their efforts. Everything was going well until a huge group of marchers, waving Union flags, made its way onto the Square.

The disgusting scenes that followed were all documented online as it happened.[36] Sectarian songs were sung, Nazi salutes were made near the Cenotaph, Saltires were set on fire and people were beaten up. There was even an attempt to set fire to the offices of the Sunday Herald, the only newspaper that claimed to support independence.[37] A young girl had a Saltire ripped from her hands while she was on the ground[38] and mounted police had to keep the thugs away from trapped independence supporters. Some pictures looked as if they had been taken in a battle zone, rather than in the centre of Glasgow.[39]

Our media, of course, could not admit that Unionists were causing the trouble. The BBC reported things as if both sides were battling, with the police caught in the middle.[40] The only way to find out the truth as it unfolded was online.[41]

The way our Fourth Estate reported the trouble, when it finally got round to admitting that the Unionist side was to blame, would lead one to believe that a gang of drunken Rangers supporters fell out of the Louden and

Blundered into George Square. It appears, however, that far-right groups from England were involved, as well as Loyalists from Northern Ireland.[42] But the ones involved are not really the issue; the main point to consider is that the whole thing was organised.[43] The person whose Facebook page I looked at, for example, lives in Edinburgh.

That night in Glasgow showed up the lies of the Unionists about the independence campaign. Nazi salutes, bigoted songs, violence against the public and a concerted effort at intimidation were all in evidence. It was, in one event, a mirror-image of everything that the Unionists had been asserting about the independence campaigners.

For those supporting independence, on the other hand, that night was a turning point. It exposed everything they were up against and provided a potent symbol of the depths to which the Unionists would sink. It also provided an image that is becoming as iconic as the student facing up to the tanks in Tiananmen Square: two young girls defiantly holding a Saltire in front of the snarling, Unionist thugs.

Of course, not everyone that was still undecided about which way to vote was going to be convinced by a smear campaign; even one of this magnitude. The sheer lack of evidence to suggest that Alex Salmond was a would-be dictator, that the SNP was full of Nazis and that there was a campaign of intimidation being orchestrated by the SNP could cause electors to question the validity of these claims. The whole plan could easily backfire if people realised what a load of garbage these claims actually were.

Another mode of attack was needed; one that would appeal to the intellectual snobbery of those that deemed themselves too clever to fall for all the spin being thrown at them in the media. And, of course, this other plan had already been put together.

Many commentators, rather patronisingly, said that the

whole independence campaign was appealing to the hearts, not the heads, of the Scottish voter. 2014 was the 700th anniversary of the Battle of Bannockburn, conjuring up apparent visions of ancient fights against the hated English. This was supposedly a direct appeal to the 'Braveheart' mentality; even though William Wallace, whether portrayed by Mel Gibson or not, was dead well before Bannockburn!

2014 was also the 100th anniversary of the start of the First World War. This, of course, could be used to foster claims of 'standing together against a common enemy' in order to help the Unionist side. It was going to be a battle of the wars; Robert the Bruce versus Lord Kitchener!

4

War Wars

Stirling is probably the most important city in Scotland historically. It was always a strategically important place and was fought over continuously throughout Scotland's history. The Old Town contains as many interesting nooks and crannies as that of Edinburgh, including a castle that has seen far more action than its more famous counterpart. The city also boasts, arguably, the oldest pub in Scotland in the Settle Inn. (*pace* Edinburgh, but claiming that there was an inn on the site way back does not exactly cut it!)

Two of the most important battles in Scotland's history also occurred in the area. The Battle of Stirling Bridge took place just below the castle in 1297, while in 1314 Robert the Bruce defeated the army of Edward II at nearby Bannockburn.

Obviously, there would be celebrations during the 700th anniversary of the battle in 2014, just as there had been celebrations during the 600th anniversary.[1] Such an undertaking is usually planned well in advance and so it was with the Bannockburn commemorations. It was in May 2010 that Alex Salmond, as Scotland's First Minister, announced that there would be a second 'Year of Homecoming' in 2014, to build on the success of the first one held in 2009.[2] There was going to be a lot going on in 2014, what with the Commonwealth Games being held in Glasgow and golf's Ryder Cup taking place at Gleneagles. It seemed the ideal time to hold another Year of Homecoming.

The 2009 Year of Homecoming had been criticised relentlessly for its portrayal of Scotland as a land of tartan, haggis, whisky and clans.[3] It seemed as if the event was pandering to a tourist-friendly idea of Scotland, rather than the real nation of nowadays. The SNP Scottish Government was blamed, George Foulkes saying, 'Homecoming has always been an expensive exercise in nationalist propaganda at the taxpayers' expense.'[4]

Of course, the critics had a point. The main event of the celebrations was a clan gathering in Edinburgh, with Highland games and the rest in Holyrood Park. To the majority of, and possibly all, Scots the idea of clans has no relevance whatsoever. It is the preserve of the American tourist, walking down the Royal Mile, clutching a certificate to show he is a member of a Scottish clan, even though his name is Schmidt, while wearing a kilt in his clan's 'ancient' tartan, which was invented in the 19th Century. It is harmless nonsense, akin to folk dressing up as cowboys in America.

The idea that having a clan gathering would somehow be effective propaganda for the SNP was just as nonsensical. Mention clan chiefs and one is immediately reminded of the Highland Clearances. The clan chiefs were also part of the nobility that gave up Scottish independence for a few quid and a seat in the House of Lords. The current chiefs that are still in Scotland, meanwhile, are Tories to a man. All-in-all the whole clan thing is hardly conducive to making folk support the SNP.

The truth is that Homecoming Scotland was the brainchild of the previous Labour administration at Holyrood. The whole shortbread-tin approach was actually just a continuation of what they had started. (Remember Jack McConnell in that hideous, pinstripe kilt?) It was rather disingenuous, therefore, for the likes of George Foulkes to claim that it was an exercise in nationalist propaganda. In fact, it was an outright lie for him to say that it 'always' had been, since it was his party that had set the whole thing up.

The 2014 Homecoming Scotland event, however, was all in the hands of the SNP; so the critics would be able to have a field day. As soon as it was announced that the referendum vote on Scottish independence would take place in September 2014 heads started to nod smugly; this time there was no doubt that the whole thing was going to be, as George Foulkes had said of the last one, nationalist propaganda.

This time round it was not the gathering of the clans that was suspicious, but its cancellation. This was nothing short of a volte-face on the part of the critics. From accusing the SNP of using all the tourist-shop imagery as propaganda for its own ends, they now accused them of playing down the tartan tat for the same purposes. As the New Statesman would have it, 'A proposed gathering of Scottish clans was cancelled, not least because they didn't fit a narrative pitting all of Scotland against England.'[5] There were mutterings too from the clan chiefs:

The event will see a re-enactment of the Battle of Bannockburn on its 700th anniversary in June as its centrepiece. But the organisers have already faced criticism for axing the clan gathering so that the re-enactment of the battle can be made the main event.'[6]

The truth was that there were no cynical motives involved in this cancellation; at least, not on the part of the SNP. It was Stirling Council that actually called off the clan gathering as early as October 2012, saying that the city would not be able to cope with the expected 30,000 that would be turning up.[7] This reasoning is important to remember, as is the fact that Stirling Council's SNP administration had been replaced by a Labour and Conservative coalition in May 2012.

Now, it could not have escaped the notice of Alex Salmond and the SNP that 2014, as well as being the 700th anniversary of the Battle of Bannockburn, was the 100th anniversary of the beginning of the First World War. Plans were already being drawn up to commemorate this event throughout the UK. Of course, the accusations were soon flying around that the Scottish Government was dragging its heels in joining in these plans.

Scotland On Sunday had this to say in April 2013:

Last October, Prime Minister David Cameron, announced more than £50m had been allocated for a "historic" commemoration of the centenary of the start of the First World War...Among the projects announced by the Prime Minister were a "massive" transformation of the Imperial War Museum, a major programme of national commemorative events "properly funded and given the proper status they deserve" and an educational programme "to create an enduring legacy for generations to come".

So far in Scotland £1m has been allocated by the Scottish Government to renovate war memorials and a panel of experts, led by former army chaplain Norman Drummond, has been tasked with coming up with a programme of events to mark the anniversary.

Meanwhile, SNP ministers have allocated £5m towards the National Trust for Scotland's new Bannockburn visitor centre and £250,000 towards the Battle of Bannockburn re-enactment event.'[8]

The accusation was that the SNP was looking to use the Bannockburn celebrations for political capital, while trying to play down the UK-wide commemoration of the Great War. As the ubiquitous George Foulkes put it, 'The First World War was very much about the Union and different parts of the UK standing together whereas Bannockburn was, of course, about fighting the English.'[9] While Labour M.P. Ann McKechin said, 'There has been a lot of emphasis from the Scottish Government on Bannockburn for political reasons but these events should not be a political football.'[10]

These reminders that the First World War was fought by the whole United Kingdom might have been meant to be damning, but another, unintended, inference could be drawn. If the UK Government wanted to commemorate the UK's involvement in the Great War, then surely the UK Government should be paying for it! The Bannockburn celebration was to be part of Homecoming

Scotland, an event to encourage Scottish tourism and sell Scotland around the world; something that was within the remit of the Scottish Government and was accounted for within the block grant given to Holyrood by Westminster. If the UK Government wanted Scotland to spend money on First World War commemorations, then it would have to provide more funds. As it was, the obviously London-centric element of the Westminster commemoration, refurbishing the Imperial War Museum, hardly implied a UK-wide perspective.

While Scottish politicians were complaining about the SNP playing 'political football' with the Bannockburn and WWI commemorations, they neglected to raise these concerns in either the Scottish or Westminster parliament. Instead, they held a cross-party meeting, from which the SNP was excluded, to discuss the matter. At this meeting they asked the Scottish Secretary, Michael Moore, to take charge of organising WWI commemoration events in Scotland; obviously the SNP Government was not to be trusted.[11]

So, while casting aspersions against the Scottish Government, pro-Union politicians were holding meetings behind its back. This kind of sneaky, backstairs conspiring would normally be condemned by all, but our media was on hand to make it seem as if there was nothing else they could do in the face of a cynical SNP. And there was worse to come.

Veterans Day was instituted in the UK in 2006. It was intended to honour those that lived through Britain's wars and conflicts; unlike Remembrance Day, which was to remember the dead. In 2009 it was changed to Armed Forces Day and became all about support for the armed services, past and present. Each year a different town or city is chosen to host the main event, while other events take place throughout the UK.

2014, as well as being the anniversary of Bannockburn and the start of WWI, was the 70th anniversary of D-Day.

It was generally expected that the choice of host would reflect this and that one of the ports on the south coast of England would be selected. It was something of a surprise, therefore, when it was announced, in August 2013, that the venue was going to be Stirling.

Sceptics might believe that this was a cynical ploy to influence voters in the upcoming referendum; and they would be right. UK Defence Secretary Philip Hammond came straight out with it, saying that it would, 'remind us in a very graphic way that we are stronger together. Britain, the United Kingdom and Scotland benefit from the scale and the power and the capability of our armed forces.'[12] So much for the SNP playing at 'political football'!

There could, however, be a spanner in the works. Remember how Stirling Council cancelled the gathering of the clans since it would not be able to cope with all the people and vehicles? How was it going to be able to manage a huge event like this that would be televised nationwide? This event would be taking place on the same day as the Bannockburn celebrations, which would only add to the logistic nightmare. Surprisingly, or, perhaps not, Stirling Council raised no objections. In fact, there was more to it than that; Stirling Council had actually bid to host the event.

A man called Callum Martin made an FOI request to the Ministry of Defence about Stirling's bid for Armed Forces Day in May 2014. Obviously being a civic-minded soul, he posted the reply online, on a website called 'What Do They Know'.[13] He discovered, and let the rest of us know, that Stirling Council had put in a bid to host the event on 20th December 2012. This was a mere two months after the gathering of the clans had been cancelled.

It is highly unlikely that the Stirling Provost woke up on 20th December and decided that it would be a good idea to apply to host Armed Forces Day; discussions for this bid must have taken place well in advance. It is also highly unlikely that, in the space of a few weeks, Stirling Council realised that it could accommodate a large event on that day after all! It is a pretty safe conclusion to reach that the gathering of the clans was actually cancelled to allow this bid to take place.

The Ministry of Defence was complicit in this cynical manoeuvre. As is evident from the reply sent to Callum Martin, the MoD was well aware that Armed Forces Day would clash with the Bannockburn celebrations.[14] This obviously did not deter them from choosing Stirling's as the winning bid.

When Labour and Tory councillors first joined forces in Stirling in 2012, it was quite puzzling to outside observers; and probably to those that lived in Stirling too. Surely these two parties were so diametrically opposed that it would be impossible for them to work together? The head of Stirling's Labour group, Corrie McChord, made it plain what the coalition was all about; 'It's the big question of separation,' he said.[15]

Scottish independence was not really a major concern for local council elections; obviously these desperate measures to keep out the SNP were being directed by the parties at a national level. Such unnatural alliances were forged at more than one Scottish council; there could be no possible advantage gained from this, except for the kind of mischief-making that took place at Stirling.

Of course, as it was intended to do, the planned Armed Forces Day threw the plans for the Bannockburn celebrations into disarray. The National Trust for Scotland, who had been organising the event, pulled out, fearing that the Armed Forces Day would diminish attendance at Bannockburn, meaning that they might not manage to recoup their outlay. VisitScotland had to take over and the event was cut back from three days to two, in order to reduce overheads.[16]

A committee had to be set up at Holyrood to look into this business. Predictably, it got nowhere. Nobody was going to admit to anything and the SNP had to tread carefully as the whole structure of the Unionist media would come crashing down on their heads at the slightest hint of an accusation.

It transpired at this investigation that Stirling Council did not consult anyone about their bid for Armed Forces Day and did not inform anyone either. The first that the organisers of the Bannockburn event heard of it was when the choice of Stirling for Armed Forces Day was announced in the press. All the organisers claimed that the clash with Armed Forces Day was the reason for cutting back on the Bannockburn event and for reducing the capacity.[17]

Councillor Neil Benny, Conservative Deputy Council leader, told the committee, 'When I first heard about the armed forces day national event, it was not clear that there was a clash of dates because the dates were not necessarily set. However, the MoD, which is an external agency, set the date and we did not have a choice in that.' He continued, 'I personally was not sure about the date that the MoD was going to set for the armed forces day.'[18]

This is totally at odds with the reply sent to Callum Martin from the MoD, which stated:

The MoD acknowledged Stirling's application to host the national event on 10 January 2013. Each year the date for Armed Forces Day is the last Saturday in June, as promulgated in the national calendar. Hence Armed Forces Day in 2015 will be Saturday 27 June...The initial application letter from the Provost Stirling Council informed the MoD of the anniversary of Bannockburn in June, although no specific dates were given.[19]

So, according to the MoD, they made it plain right from the start what date was penciled-in for Armed Forces Day. It is safe to assume that they would also make it plain that the date was non-negotiable. Somebody, to put it bluntly, was lying. The date for Armed Forces Day has been set for years now, so it could hardly have come as a surprise to Stirling Council what the date would be. At the same time, the MoD states that nobody at Stirling Council gave the date for the Bannockburn celebration. So either we believe Stirling Council or the MoD. It certainly gives one pause for thought when one reads that Neil Benny told the committe, 'There's no question there was any intent to try to diminish Bannockburn Live in any possible way.'[20]

And so the two events went head-to-head. On one side was Bannockburn Live, which was being perceived as being all about winning votes for the SNP; on the other was Armed Forces Day, which, as we have seen, was most definitely about winning votes against Scottish independence. Which one would the public go to?

The big advantage that Armed Forces Day had was that it was free; whereas Bannockburn Live was a bit on the expensive side. On the minus side, however, was the fact that if you have seen one supersonic aeroplane flying overhead, you have seen them all! Today's children need a bit more than a few planes, a couple of military bands, some soldiers marching about and a plastic flag to wave to get them excited. Bannockburn Live, on the other hand, was offering involvement, which would obviously be more attractive to most youngsters.

As it turned out, Bannockburn Live was a sell-out, with many folk having to be turned away at the gate.[21] To be fair, though, it was not a complete success; there have been complaints about the massive queues and it seems that the venue probably was not quite big enough.[22]

It was claimed that Armed Forces Day attracted 35,000 people, although those figures are disputed. In fact, many believed that the crowd was nowhere near that size and provided evidence to prove their point.[23] Whatever the truth, it did not reflect well on Stirling Council. Either they attracted a fraction of what they were claiming, in which case they were lying; or they did attract as many as they said, in which case they were lying when they cancelled the clans gathering!

Since the perception was that the Bannockburn

celebration was merely a political tool of the SNP, attempts were made to downplay the significance of the battle. It was called a 'daft medieval scrimmage'[24] and some tried to deny that it had anything to do with Scottish independence at all; it was just part of a power struggle among the nobility.[25] That would make it not much different from every other battle and war in Europe in the Middle Ages, so perhaps they are all of no real importance. The Declaration of Arbroath was dismissed in the same sneering manner.[26] There was nothing in it for the ordinary people, only the nobility.

As fate would have it, 2015 sees the 800th anniversary of the signing of Magna Carta. Any real analysis of this document shows that it was solely concerned with the nobility getting one over on King John.[27] It had nothing whatsoever to do with democracy or universal freedoms; in fact, the majority of the English population was not covered by its provisions.

The document did not even manage to do what it was meant to do: limit the powers of the king to act arbitrarily and guarantee the rights and liberties of the Church and nobility. One only has to look at the reign of Henry VIII for proof as he looted the Church's property and capriciously cut the heads off noblemen for being *too* Protestant. In fact it was not until the Bill of Rights was passed in 1689 that royal power was finally curbed.[28]

This, however, is not what we will be bombarded with in 2015. Magna Carta has taken on a mythical quality and is often cited as the beginnings of democracy; not just in England but in the United States and elsewhere. It is held up as one of the greatest milestones in history, even though its influence as a symbol is far more important than its content. We will be told, throughout 2015, how this document is the ultimate guarantor of all our rights and liberties;[29] while the Declaration of Arbroath is relegated to the position of an unimportant footnote in history.

The hypocrisy of this stance against the Declaration and the Battle of Bannockburn is even more evident when it is compared to what we are told about the First World War. The Scottish Wars of Independence were just for the benefit of a narrow, aristocratic oligarchy; WWI, on the other hand was all about fighting 'in the name of freedom'[30] and to defend western democracy from the expansionism of Germany.[31] Strangely, nobody bothers to mention that over half of the men going off to fight in 1914 did not have the vote. So what made them any different from the ordinary men that fought for Wallace and Bruce?

There was also the allegation that the celebrations of the Battle of Bannockburn were of an anti-English nature. Scottish Labour MP Ian Davidson said that the commemoration of Bannockburn was to celebrate 'the murder of hundreds of thousands of English people.'[32] While our old friend, Simon Winder, says:

In what sense is this (commemorating Bannockburn) any different from commemorating Tannenberg or Kosovo Polje? The atavistic anti-Englishness is no less horrible and mad than the anti-Russian or anti-Muslim connotations of these other two examples.'[33]

Surely the same accusations could be leveled at the commemorations for the anniversary of the First World War? This is especially true given Michael Gove's insistence that Germany was the villain of the piece in the Great War.[34] All the emphasis on fighting for freedom against German aggression is bound to anger the Germans; after all, Britain was just as aggressive, expansionist and imperialist as Germany. Then again, maybe the powers-that-be in Britain just do not care what Germany thinks!

And so, while condemning the SNP for supposedly using a battle to win votes, the Unionists were perfectly happy to use perhaps the worst war in history to do exactly what they were accusing the SNP of. Not only that, but they lied and finagled their way into having the Armed Forces Day in exactly the same place at exactly the same time as the Bannockburn celebrations. Were there any depths to which they would not sink?

In January 2012 Johann Lamont, the leader of Scottish Labour, had this to say about the upcoming referendum: 'There will be a Labour campaign that will be making the point about why you would want to stay strong within the United Kingdom.'[35] It sounded as if the intended campaign was going to be all about the positive benefits of remaining in the Union; so what went wrong? All this smearing, lying and shady, backstairs dealing was hardly what you could call positive; in fact, you would be hard-pushed to even call it a campaign! Still, as long as it was effective nobody was going to care what you called it.

There was, however, a problem. In every election campaign there are always those pain-in-the-arse folk that insist on wanting to know things that the politicians would rather not go into. These people are not interested in who is best-looking, who wears the best suit or whose party used to support the Nazis; they want to know exactly what they are voting for. The SNP had already set out its stall so all these voters needed now was to know why they should remain in the Union. Better Together was going to have to come up with some counter-proposals to the SNP's plans

5

Sterling Stuff

Johann Lamont might have been planning a positive campaign but, unfortunately, either she forgot to tell anyone else or they had decided not to listen to her. Whatever the reason, Better Together mounted a campaign that, instead of explaining why we should stay part of the UK, merely tried to frighten us with stories of what would happen if we were to vote YES.

The main attacks were all about money, of course. The SNP had set out a plan to still use Sterling in an independent Scotland, as part of a currency union with the remainder of the UK. Better Together ridiculed this idea; apparently such a scheme was impossible and Alistair Darling and the rest started to constantly demand to know what the 'Plan B' was.

The reason why Scotland could not use Sterling had nothing to do with logistics or anything; rather it was down to the pettiness of the powers-that-be in Westminster. Like some selfish, petulant brat, the three main UK parties all announced that they would not allow an independent Scotland to use the Pound and that they would have nothing to do with any currency union. It was their ball and nobody else was getting to play with it!

Essentially what the Unionists were doing was putting obstacles in the way of independence and then disingenuously making out that these obstacles were something natural and would just appear out of nowhere. It was a petty game to play and, conversely, showed that an independent Scotland was perfectly viable. If it was not feasible then they would hardly need to put obstacles in the way, would they?

The governor of the Bank of England, Mark Carney, said that 'a currency required a centralised bank and shared banking regulations. Common taxation and spending were also needed.'[1] Obviously this man has never heard of the

Euro, and he is supposed to be the biggest hot-shot banker in the world!

He explained further that with any form of fiscal arrangement you 'need tax, revenues and spending flowing across those borders to help equalise, to an extent, some of the inevitable differences.'[2] This, of course, is disingenuous in the extreme. If all these measures were needed to make the currency work then the obvious and logical assumption is that they are currently in place.

At the moment there is not much evidence of this 'equalising'. Most of the UK's tax money is spent in London: Thames barriers, new airports, fancy new railway stations, high-speed rail links and anything the capital's residents need to make life easier. Start traveling north and this up-to-date infrastructure seems to disappear. People lose their houses in floods, public transport is overcrowded, as are the roads; the money to make things better, however, is just not available.

In fact, the figures for this overspending on the capital are startling. £14.5billion is being spent on the new Crossrail project, compared to just £1.6billion on rail projects for the whole of the north of England. Infrastructure expenditure in London in 2013 amounted to £5,426 per person, while the per capita spending in the north-east of England came in at a paltry £223.[3]

It seems that 'equalisation' is hardly a priority at present so why should it suddenly become one if Scotland were to leave the UK? At present it seems that all the taxes in the UK flow down to London and are spent there. Perhaps the real concern of Mark Carney is that the loss of taxes on oil revenues might mean a cut in expenditure in the capital!

Alistair Darling leapt on Carney's statements to argue that'...a currency union is not compatible with sovereignty. It would mean what would then be a foreign country having control over our economy. That's why a currency union would be bad for Scotland, as well as the rest of the UK.'[4]

Darling neglects to explain exactly how this would be bad for Scotland. The fact is that London dictates our economy while we are in the UK; so is that bad for Scotland? What possible difference would it make if England became a 'foreign country'? It shows how ridiculous Darling's argument is. It also, however, begs the question as to the point of Scotland becoming independent if things are just going to be the same. Time for a reality check.

The fact of the matter is that the Government, whether in Edinburgh or Westminster, has no real control over the economy anymore; it is debatable if they ever did. Planned economies ended up being abject failures. The UK Government used to follow Keynes's ideas until, inexplicably, inflation and unemployment both increased at the same time. Thatcher's monetarist policies met the same, ignominious, fate. Eventually governments pretty much gave up and abandoned Sterling to the vagaries of the markets.

All the Bank of England can do is react to whatever is happening to Sterling; it has no real control. It desperately manipulates interest rates to stimulate growth or to curb spending depending on what is happening to the Pound in the markets. It is hardly what you could call controlling the economy.

So if some future independent Scottish government decided to increase public spending to improve services and create jobs, there would not be a thing the Westminster Government or the Bank of England could do about it. That is assuming, of course, that the currency union came about, which the Unionist side was adamant was never going to happen.

The truth is, however, that Westminster and Better Together had jumped the gun just to get one up on the independence campaigners. They knew as well as Alex Salmond that a currency union was an inevitability; all that was uncertain were the details that would be negotiated when the time came.

As Better Together kept telling us, most of Scotland's trade was with England. If Scotland became independent it is doubtful that English manufacturers that sell to Scotland, and traders that bought Scottish products, would be entirely happy about having to deal in a different currency. The pressure would be on the Westminster Government to agree to currency union and there would be hell to pay if they refused.

The big problem for those against a currency union is the current strength of the Pound, which shows no sign of abating. A strong Pound might seem great when you are away on holiday and you can get a lot more sangria for your Sterling. It also means, however, that people abroad cannot afford British products, which in turn leads to loss of jobs. Would the Westminster Government allow the decline of English companies because Scottish customers could not afford their products, simply for the sake of a principle?

A couple of commentators, including the Rector of Edinburgh University, argued that Westminster is in favour of a strong Pound because that is what the banks want.[5] It is doubtful that this would change if Scotland were to become independent; the London markets would continue to deal heavily in Sterling, keeping it a strong currency. The only way that Westminster could protect English manufacturers that sell to Scotland, then, would be to agree to a currency union.

In March 2014 an unnamed government minister let the cat out of the bag, saying that a currency union would be agreed. He or she said, 'There would be a highly complex set of negotiations after a yes vote, with many moving pieces. The UK wants to keep Trident nuclear weapons at Faslane and the Scottish government wants a currency union – you can see the outlines of a deal.'[6] You certainly could! You could also see that Nicola Sturgeon was right about the continual refusal to even contemplate a currency union as being nothing more than 'bluff and bluster'.[7]

Of course, not everyone campaigning for Scottish independence was keen on the idea of using the Pound or in having a currency union; some folk favoured the Euro while others were all for Scotland having its own currency. If Scotland were to become independent then there was every

74

chance that one of these ideas would come to fruition; after all, once the country was independent we could vote for whoever we wanted.

This fact, however, was completely ignored by the media. In keeping with their focus on the SNP to the exclusion of all others involved in the independence campaign, they presented it as a straight fight between the quixotic Alex Salmond and the wiser heads of Better Together. And since the media were determined that a currency union would never happen, they constantly badgered Salmond to reveal his 'Plan B'. Salmond, meanwhile, refused to divulge this and stuck to his guns that a currency union was the best solution.

The whole thing about a 'Plan B', however, is not letting anyone know about it. For most of us the only time we have to think about a 'Plan A' and 'Plan B' is during the teenage mating game. We have all been in that position where we might ask somebody out but have another somebody lined up in case the first one turns us down. Can you imagine, though, what would happen if you let your first choice know about your second and vice-versa?

'Hello, Mary? Do you fancy going out on Saturday? That's great! I don't know if I can make it, though. I'm going to ask Jenny Simpson out, but she might say no and I thought I'd better check that you were free in case I have to settle for you. I'm going to phone Jenny now so I'll let you know what's happening later on!'

'Hello, Jenny? Do you fancy going out on Saturday? I need to know now so I can let Mary Wilson know. I asked her out first in case you said no and she'll want to know what's happening.'

This sixteen-year-old lad would be lucky to make it to his seventeenth birthday, never mind make it out on a date. Mary would hardly be best pleased at being nothing more than a 'back up', while Jenny might decide to leave him hanging to see how keen he is to go out with her. It is not a good idea to let anyone know what alternative plans you have.

I remember when I was at university a friend of mine ended up not being offered a place on campus in his final year. I accompanied him to the accommodation office, advising him to argue that he would not be able to do his dissertation if he was off-campus, since he needed easy access to the library and the university laboratories, as well as a computer. (This was back in the 1980s) He argued his point eloquently but then made the mistake of filling in a form for off-campus accommodation 'just in case'. I slapped my forehead in frustration since he had as much as admitted that he would be prepared to settle for second-best. Of course, the result was that he was given a room in a flat a few miles off-campus.

Alex Salmond was in exactly the same position. If he were to even hint at the possibility of settling for another currency solution then it would only serve to strengthen the resolve of those opposed to a currency union. Only as a last resort, when all possibility of a currency union had gone, would he announce what his 'Plan B' was.

Mark Carney was playing the same game when it came to the possibility of savers moving their funds out of Scottish banks. He said, 'It's never a good idea to talk about contingency plans in public, other than to assure people that we have them, and I just underscore in terms of our responsibilities for financial stability we do have a wide range of tools and plans.'[8]

Carney was portrayed as being shrewd and clever, as anyone would be that played his cards close to his chest. Salmond, on the other hand, was cast as an ignorant, intransigent buffoon, who obviously did not know the first thing about economics, even though he has a degree in the subject and worked as an economist for the Scottish Office and the Royal Bank of Scotland.

Again and again in the media we were told that a currency union was not going to happen, while Salmond insisted that Westminster was bluffing. The two sides were staring each other out, waiting to see who was going to blink first. Salmond refused to give any details of contingency plans, while Westminster indignantly denied that they were bluffing. It must be said, though, that it would not be much of a bluff if they were to admit that they were bluffing!

While castigating and harassing Alex Salmond and the SNP, the media never once questioned Westminster or Better Together about their contingency plans. What was Westminster going to do to help safeguard English companies that depended on Scotland for their business in the event of Scotland voting YES? How were they going to budget for the loss of oil and gas tax revenues? How would the markets react to Sterling no longer having the backing of North Sea oil and gas? What was Westminster doing to offset the possible detrimental effects on Sterling in the markets? All valid questions; but none of them were asked.

As Mark Carney said, you do not divulge contingency plans. With Better Together it was a case of wait-and-see; they would deal with independence as and when it happened. Nobody bothered to question Scots Tories, Labour or Liberal Democrats about how they would react to an independent Scotland; would their parties stand for election to an independent Scottish parliament? If any of them ended up running Scotland, would they not prefer to have closer economic links with Westminster in a currency union?

Any contingency plans that Scottish politicians in Better Together had were allowed to remain a secret; Alex Salmond and the SNP, however, were not allowed this luxury. All the demands to know 'Plan B' were calculated to undermine the position of the independence campaign; putting the SNP in an almost unwinnable position as far as the media were concerned. If they divulged their contingency plans then they would lose their bargaining position; whereas keeping such plans a secret brought a barrage of contemptuous accusations that the SNP had no idea what they were doing.

It could be argued that Alex Salmond and the SNP were the ones looking for change so the other side had no questions to answer; they were simply campaigning to keep the status quo. The fact remains, however, that Better Together and the media were the ones making such a huge deal about contingency plans. It appeared, though, that only one side was expected to have them.

As well as questions over which currency an independent Scotland would use, there was also ostensible concern over how the country was going to pay for everything. Scotland was much better-off within the UK, went the argument; it was going to struggle financially without the crutch of the Barnett Formula.

The Barnett Formula determines how much each of the devolved parliaments receives each year for spending on services that they are responsible for. You take how much is being spent in England, double it, add ten, halve it, take away the number you first thought of and Bob's your uncle. Better Together, the media and Westminster never tired of telling us how well Scotland did out of it.

It certainly seemed that way. In 2013 Scotland got £10,152 per capita, Wales £9,709 and England £8,529.[2] Why on earth should we want to leave the Union when we were in receipt of such bounty?

Such figures are constantly being quoted to let us know that the English taxpayer is subsidising us here in Scotland. Unsurprisingly, people in England are outraged; why should they be paying taxes so that the Scots can get free prescriptions? There are calls for money to be given to areas on the basis of need, rather than geography; with Wales and the north of England feeling particularly aggrieved. But is their anger being directed at the right target?

These figures that are thrust under our noses are, in the case of England, an average and averages can be deceptive. The current UK average wage, for example, is £26,500 per year.[10] This figure, however, is made artificially high with the inclusion of the obscenely high salaries of footballers, company chairmen, bankers etc. In the same way, the average expenditure in England does not show the true picture.

We have already seen how London gets the lion's share of expenditure when it comes to money being spent in England.

As was pointed out in the Guardian, 'Londoners receive more taxpayer money on health, housing and culture – and they get more than double the national average on transport.'[11] And those figures are based on the UK average, rather than just England; so more is spent per capita in London than in Scotland. It would seem that the majority of the money earmarked for England is being lavished on London, to the detriment of the other English regions.

But, so the argument goes, London pays more tax than any other area of Britain; surely that should be reflected in how that tax money is spent?[12] Scotland, meanwhile, gets more spent on it than it puts in. The figures generally given by the Treasury in London is that Scotland contributes 8.2% of the total UK tax revenue but receives 9.3% of UK spending.[13]

This disparity is what has got the English, not to mention the Welsh, riled. It also provided ammunition for the pro-Unionist campaigners since it proved that Scotland would be unable to manage outside the UK. There is, however, a major discrepancy in these figures.

Since oil and gas were first discovered in the North Sea, successive Westminster governments have refused to include tax revenues from this source as part of Scotland's contribution to the UK. If it is included then Scotland provides 9.9% of the UK's tax revenue.[14] It is not difficult to see why Westminster excludes the oil tax revenue; it is a cynical method of making it look as if England is subsidising Scotland. It also takes everyone's eye off the massive public spending in London!

The argument against an independent Scotland being able to survive financially, then, is based on a lie. By any international standard, the North Sea oil and gas fields are in Scottish waters, no matter how Westminster tries to spin it. Any claims that said fields belonged to the UK and should be divided up accordingly would find about as much international support as the UK claims on the Suez Canal in 1956.

But there was apparently another problem. According to the Office for Budget Responsibility oil and gas production in the North Sea was in decline.[15] This would mean less revenue for an independent Scotland and necessitate either spending cuts or an increase in other taxes.

The SNP disputed that things were as bad as was being made out; but, then, you could hardly expect them to say otherwise. Essentially, Westminster and Better Together were lying, according to the SNP; surely the UK Government would not behave like that? The truth is that the UK Government had lied before about North Sea oil; in fact, it had continued to lie for decades.

In the early-to-mid 1970s the extraction of oil and gas from beneath the North Sea was in its infancy. Obviously the UK Government wanted reports on the revenues that could be gleaned from this source, as well as the impact that it would have on the economy. One such report was presented by Professor Gavin McCrone in 1974. McCrone had been tasked with looking into the effect that North Sea oil and gas would have on Scotland if it were to become independent. The results of his investigations proved to be alarming to the Heath Government.

McCrone's findings showed that the Government was massively underestimating the future revenues that would be available. He even showed that the SNP's estimates erred largely on the side of caution. If Scotland became independent it would become one of the richest countries in the world. This was a worrying development as far as Westminster was concerned. The SNP had been making significant headway during the 1970s; if the Scottish public were to learn the truth about the possible wealth available to them then independence might be inevitable.

The Government, perhaps understandably, marked the report 'Top Secret' and buried it. The subsequent governments of Wilson, Callaghan, Thatcher, Major and Blair all followed suit; nobody, especially the Scottish electorate, was to know of this document.[16] Meanwhile, officially projected revenue figures were kept low; as far as anyone knew, North Sea oil and gas were not the bonanza that the SNP was claiming.

Professor McCrone believes that the low projections were a mistake on the part of the Government and that no political motives were behind it. Even if we give the Westminster Government the benefit of the doubt, once the big money started to roll in then it was obvious that they had been wrong. No effort, however, was made to revise the figures.

Dennis Healey claims that the decisions were made in a more cynically deliberate way. He says:

I think we did underplay the value of the oil to the country because of the threat of nationalism but that was mainly down to Thatcher. We didn't actually see the rewards from oil in my period in office because we were investing in the infrastructure rather than getting the returns and really, Thatcher wouldn't have been able to carry out any of her policies without that additional 5 per cent on GDP from oil. Incredible good luck she had from that.[17]

McCrone, in another report in 1976, advised the Government to set up an investment fund for the whole UK but that they should give 'especial priority to Scotland'. The latter advice was in order to keep the Scots sweet and keep them away from the SNP. This report was ignored. Callaghan used the initial funds to help bail out the UK, while Thatcher used the billions available in the 1980s to fund the 'economic miracle'.[18] This economic growth was mostly confined to - where else – London, while Scotland, instead of becoming the richest country in Europe, was thrown on the scrapheap.

This has to rank as one of the biggest political frauds in history; not to mention being tantamount to theft. Even under the thirty-year rule the report was not released and had to be requested under Freedom of Information laws by the SNP, making sure that the request was carefully worded to leave no room for the Government to wriggle out of it.[19]

This fraud showed the utter hypocrisy of the Westminster Government and the Better Together campaign. There were constant complaints that Alex Salmond was not revealing the full facts about Scottish independence. 'Legendary' political commentator, Tom Brown had this to say:

…the unanswered questions about an Independent Scotland have mounted up. They stall, give vague and veiled non-answers while crucial questions on economy, currency, pensions, defence and international relations are filed under 'to be negotiated'.[20]

After decades of Westminster and the UK political parties keeping the Scottish electorate in the dark, this 'legend' certainly had some brass neck!

Since Scotland had been lied to for all that time it was reasonable to question the veracity of current statements emanating from London. Perhaps the doom-laden scenario concerning North Sea oil and gas was, to put it mildly, bending the truth a little.

There is still a lot of oil out there and there are billions of pounds being invested offshore of Shetland. Official figures, of course, do not predict terribly great things from these oil and gas deposits but social media online were buzzing with rumours when David Cameron made a surprise visit to Shetland in July 2014.

This was the first visit of a UK prime minister to Shetland in thirty-four years. It was not reported in the media, it came completely out of the blue and was shrouded in secrecy. A story started to emerge that BP had made discoveries in its Clair Ridge project that had 'far exceeded expectations'.[21] The fact that BP refused to comment added fuel, if you will pardon the pun, to these speculations.

Accompanying the Prime Minister was Alistair Carmichael, the Scottish Secretary and MP for Orkney and Shetland. He dismissed the rumours out of hand, saying:

These rumours are quite ridiculous. If there was any truth in this suggestion that there has been a massive oil discovery and that it was being kept secret, then surely the last thing the Prime Minister would do would be visiting where you could only draw attention to it.'[22]

He gave no reason for the Prime Minister's visit and none has been forthcoming since. His assertion that the visit would 'draw attention' to any supposed 'massive oil discovery' is disingenuous; what better way to conceal matters than for the Prime Minister to go himself, allowing Carmichael to present this argument. It sounds unrealistically devious but, as we have discovered, the Westminster Government is not above this kind of thing.

Stories that all the workers on Clair Ridge were sent home until September[23] perhaps provide a possible explanation of what was going on. It is quite plausible to suggest that, although no discoveries had been made as yet, Cameron wanted to make sure than none were forthcoming before the referendum. If a massive discovery were to be made then it would be difficult to prevent the news from leaking out. It would be prudent, therefore, to suspend operations until a NO vote was firmly in the bag.

But why would Cameron go himself? Well, apart from the possible double-bluff outlined above, it is possible, indeed probable, that he did not entirely trust anyone else at that time. Remember, it had only been a short time before that one of his ministers had anonymously admitted that a currency union was a distinct possibility. Who was to say that the same thing would not happen if he sent another minister on this assignment? Quite possibly the details of his visit were unknown even to his cabinet colleagues.

Of course, it was not long after the referendum that an announcement was made of the discovery of a new oil field in the North Sea off Shetland. BP and GDF Suez described the new find as 'encouraging'.[24] It would appear, then, that Westminster is continuing the policy of deceit and disinformation that it began in the 1970s.

A further example of the Westminster Government's mendacity emerged in May 2014. The UK Treasury estimated that it would cost a new, independent Scottish government £2.7bn to set up all the new government departments it would need. This figure was later revised to £1.5bn. They extrapolated this sum from figures provided by Professor Patrick Dunleavy, of the London School of Economics.

Professor Dunleavy, however, claimed that they had manipulated his figures and said that the real start-up costs would be in the region of £150m - £200m, a fraction of what the Treasury was projecting.[25]

Another academic was dragged into this web of deceit, Professor Robert Young of Western Ontario University. He had exactly the same story to tell as Professor Dunleavy; the Treasury was misusing his figures. He had worked on the cost of Quebec seceding from Canada, for which his team had provided various estimates. The Treasury figure for Scotland was extrapolated from the top estimate in his report; the lowest estimate, which the Treasury was obviously ignoring, would be £600m.[26]

Westminster had been caught out yet again. While Better Together was lambasting the independence campaign, accusing it of not providing answers, their own answers were based on lies supplied by Westminster. Not that the media were overly keen to let us know about this. The story of these lies never made the front page; that was reserved for accusing Alex Salmond of doing precisely what Westminster and Better Together were doing: lying!

And so we come to the next component of the Better Together campaign aimed at those that demanded details. This was about what life would be like in an independent Scotland. With no currency, no revenue and the loss of the generous Barnett Formula, Scotland would not be able to afford to spend anywhere near as much as it was doing at present. We were all going to be jobless, ill and starving within a few, short years and would be begging on our bended knees to be allowed back into the United Kingdom!

6

Unwell and Unemployed

In June 2014 the author JK Rowling gave a donation of £1m to Better Together and wrote on her blog about her concerns regarding an independent Scotland. She did not outline what these concerns were, merely going on about 'risks'. One thing she did feel strongly about, however, was the possibility that there would not be enough investment in medical research in an independent Scotland.[1]

She was echoing concerns expressed by medical researchers themselves. Several of these boffins signed an open letter telling of their worries about medical research funding if Scotland were to 'sleepwalk' into independence.[2] By using such an emotive word as 'sleepwalk' it was obvious that they felt that the rest of us were not as clever or as well-informed as they were! Perhaps if they spent less time worrying about their grants and more time on actual research they would have nothing to worry about. Then again, if they were to actually produce some results they would be out of a job!

The SNP had put forward the idea that an independent Scotland could have a common research fund with what was left of the UK. There is already a precedent for such a scheme; UK universities already work closely with their counterparts in Ireland and joint funding was already in place. Why could such a scheme not be extended to an independent Scotland? Simple; Westminster refused point-blank to countenance it.[3] The excuse given by the professors for Westminster's intransigence was that they would not want to be involved in funding a competitor. If these scientists see their research as being a competition then perhaps it is time they sought funding from the private sector!

JK Rowling's blog post and the medical researchers' open

letter would suggest that everything is hunky-dory with research funding at the present time; it is, however, manifestly not. There is another open letter online, which appeared in October 2014, expressing the grave concerns of scientists throughout Europe at the cuts in funding in all countries.[4] (I wonder if the ones supporting Better Together have signed it; or perhaps their jobs are secure now so they do not care!)

JK Rowling, of course, would argue that the lack of funding in the UK was down to the present Government; once her friends in the Labour Party were back in power things would be very different. The truth is, however, that she made a huge donation to the Multiple Sclerosis Society Scotland in 2006 and then another £10m in 2010;[5] why would this be necessary if the Labour Government had been providing adequate funds during the previous thirteen years?

Rowling's concerns about this future funding was, therefore, rather specious. There has been a serious lack of funding for medical and scientific research in the UK, no matter who has been in power; so why should she be concerned about the same thing happening in an independent Scotland? Surely she could just get her chequebook out again? Her reasons do not appear to be reasons at all, but rationalisations; one cannot help but wonder what her real reasons are.

It was not just the funding for research that there was concern about; it was the whole NHS. Most of the concern in this respect came from the pro-independence side. This concern was in regard to the increasing involvement of the private sector in the NHS in England; something Labour was apparently fighting hard against.[6] As Better Together pointed out, the NHS in Scotland was the responsibility of the Scottish Government, so was safe from whatever might happen in England. The only one that could privatise the NHS in Scotland was Alex Salmond, as Gordon Brown pointed out.[7] This argument, however, was completely disingenuous.

The way the Barnett Formula operates is that Scotland's block grant is based on public spending in England; if less is spent on the NHS in England then Scotland gets proportionately less in its grant. It stands to reason that the more the private sector gets involved in England, the less is going to be spent by the Westminster Government. This, of course, would have a knock-on effect as far as the Barnett Formula grant to Scotland. In effect, privatisation in England would mean less money coming to Scotland. Of course, the Scottish Government could choose to keep spending on the NHS at the same level; this, however, would mean cuts elsewhere.

Better Together, of course, disputed this but no figures were presented; they merely accused the pro-independence side (or, rather, Alex Salmond) of peddling lies and disinformation. The best scare story they could come up with was that if Scotland became independent then it would destroy the current situation where 'it doesn't matter if you are from England, Wales, Northern Ireland or Scotland – patients can go to any part of the country to get the care that your condition requires.'[8] This, however, is not strictly true.

To all intents and purposes, abortion is illegal in Northern Ireland. If a woman in Northern Ireland needs to terminate her pregnancy she has to travel to the UK mainland to have it done. She will need to go to a private clinic and pay, however, since she is not entitled to have the procedure done by the NHS. When this policy was challenged in the High Court in London, the judge, Mr. Justice King, ruled that the Westminster Health Secretary's duty 'is a duty in relation to the physical and mental health of the people of England', and that duty did not extend 'to persons who are ordinarily resident in Northern Ireland.'[9]

This ruling shows that the whole idea that 'patients can go to any part of the country to get the care that your condition requires' is a fraud. It would appear that the pro-independence campaigners were right in their contention that the NHS is not homogeneous or united; in effect, receiving treatment in England if you come from Scotland depends on cross-border agreement. What was to stop this agreement continuing if Scotland were to become independent?

Eventually, Better Together was provided with a more credible argument against the pro-independence side. The Institute for Fiscal Studies came up with figures that showed that the Scottish Government was intending to cut spending on the NHS by 1.2% in 2015-2016. Meanwhile, spending on the NHS in England was set to rise by 4.4% in the same period. Not only that, but while overall cuts in England were going to be in the region of 13%, Scotland would be protected by that 4.4% spend, which would be reflected in the Barnett Formula grant to Scotland.[10]

While Better Together smugly broadcast these figures nobody, least of all the media, stopped to consider that they made no sense. The Barnett Formula is intimately tied to spending in England; if there were going to be 13%-worth of cuts in England, then Scotland's grant would be cut accordingly. If the 4.4% was going to reduce the effect of these cuts in Scotland's grant then it must, necessarily, reduce the effect of the cuts in England. At best the figures were muddle-headed; at worst, a downright lie!

These figures, although touted as such by Better Together did nothing whatsoever to show that Scotland's NHS was safer within the UK. All they did was demonstrate that Scotland's spending budget was irrevocably dependent on the vagaries of the Westminster Government. There was nothing at all to disprove the contention of the YES campaign that the NHS in Scotland would be safer if Scotland were to become independent.

There is one further consideration to take into account: where this information was coming from. The Institute for Fiscal Studies is an independent organisation, set up to provide analysis of taxation in the UK. It does not always agree with the government of the day; in fact, right-wing politicians see it as a hotbed of socialism, while left-wing commentators deride it as a tool of the Establishment. It pays to remember, however, that both right and left of the political spectrum were supporting the maintenance of the Union.

Let us look back at our friends, the medical boffins, who had written the open letter about their worries. They expressed another concern to the media: that the principals of the universities in Scotland were too frightened to put their names to the letter. What they were supposed to be scared of was putting at risk their funding from the Scottish Government.[11] It is easy to dismiss this declaration as just another smear by Better Together but it is a constant terror borne by every academic that his funding might dry up and he will be out of a job. If we accept that this is the case with the university authorities in Scotland, then we must accept that the same is true with academics in England.

Concerns have been expressed before about the funding of the Institute for Fiscal Studies, which seems to mostly come from Westminster Government departments.[12] True, it also receives grants from the devolved parliaments but they will hardly be on the same scale as those coming directly or indirectly from Westminster. The IFS was often called into question for being biased[13] and yet Westminster, no matter who was in power, kept on funding it.

But there was one thing that united both sides of the House in Westminster: keeping Scotland in the UK. Is it beyond the realms of possibility that the IFS was juggling the figures to hold onto its substantial funding? Well, if we are to believe the Better Together arguments then this is an entirely plausible scenario. If they are prepared to tell us that academics in Scotland were scared of losing their funding, then the same must be true of those in England, especially in London; they cannot have it both ways.

So, according to Better Together, if Scotland became independent we were all going to suffer as far as health was concerned. There would be no more research into disease and our hospitals and medical professionals would all disappear as the funding dried up. Of course, an independent Scottish government could decide to redirect funds from other budgets to maintain our health service; we could have the choice of our kids growing up thick or growing up with rickets. No matter how an independent Scotland intended to spend its money, however, one problem remained as far as Better Together was concerned: would it actually have any money to spend?

Any government can only spend what it raises in taxes; but what if there was nobody to raise taxes from? According to Better Together, our media and everyone that supported a NO vote, there would be no jobs in an independent Scotland. We had no need to worry, therefore, about our NHS or research or education or anything. We were all going to be too busy eating each other out of sheer starvation to care!

This was perhaps the biggest part of the Better Together campaign: that there would be very little in the way of jobs if Scotland were to become independent. Businesses would relocate to England, or just pull out altogether, leaving Scotland practically destitute. No wonder the pro-independence side referred to the Better Together campaign as 'Project Fear'!

Independent think-tanks almost unanimously warned that jobs were at risk; many jobs. Ruth Porter of Policy Exchange said, 'The raft of economically incoherent policies being proposed by Alex Salmond would be disastrous for Scotland.'[14] Andrew Hilton of the Centre for the Study of Financial Innovation warned, 'If there were a Yes vote there would be utter panic - with the Scottish fund managers heading for the Border in droves.'[15] Ray Barrell of Brunel University in London warned that independence 'is the introduction of a new border. That is likely to reduce Scottish GDP by 3 per cent'.[16] If these analysts were correct then an independent Scotland would be up a particular brown-coloured creek without an adequate means of propulsion.

There is, however, a major point to consider when looking at these assertions: just how independent were these independent analysts? Policy Exchange, for example, is not linked to any government department; in fact, it is a registered charity. It is worth noting, though, that it has close links with the Conservative Party, some of its members going on to work as ministers in David Cameron's cabinet. It also has ties with the Telegraph, the Times and the Spectator; all of which are right-wing publications.[17]

Another point of interest about Policy Exchange is that it was caught up in a major scandal a few years ago. It appears that it might possibly have forged documents in order to provide evidence for its assertion that British mosques were promoting Islamic extremism.[18] It is hardly, then, an organisation that is above reproach.

Ray Barrell, of Brunel University, is, like all academics, dependent on government funding for his job. As we have previously noted, this places restraints on such academics' independence. There is also the little matter of him being an adviser to the Treasury between 1984 and 1987.[19] Again, not exactly what you would call an impartial observer.

This was one of the observations of Dr. John Robertson, whom we have already met. (See Chapter 1) If an analyst or organisation made a pro-independence observation, the media would be at pains to point out their links to the Scottish Government. Meanwhile, no such relationships were ever revealed when it came to anti-independence pronouncements. All such observations were usually presented as being 'independent', even when they manifestly were not.[20]

The other so-called independent analysts mentioned above all had strong connections with the banking sector. The other experts quoted in the Daily Mail article, moreover, were, every one of them, senior members of banks or investment organisations. Surely, though, the banking sector had no vested interest in maintaining the Union? Why would they bother to propagate fear of unemployment to prevent Scotland becoming independent?

The answer comes in a very telling quote in the same Daily Mail article. Philip Rush of Nomura, a huge Japanese financial holding company, said of Scottish independence, 'A fate similar to the secular stagnation in productivity seen in parts of Europe's socialist south may await.' As well as being an extremely simplistic and sweeping explanation of the relative poverty of southern Europe, this shows where the fear of the financial institutions lay.

Not only was the SNP putting forward a socialist programme for an independent Scotland but Scotland is known for being well to the left of England, especially southern England. Any subsequent elections in an independent Scotland would no doubt reflect this and result in socialist government after socialist government. This was the nightmare scenario that bankers wanted to avoid.

In the free-for-all that exists at present, bankers can pretty much do what they like: investing in huge risk ventures, awarding themselves massive bonuses and charging customers the earth for ridiculous things like going overdrawn by a penny. If everything goes wrong their friends in Government are ready to bail them out with taxpayers' money. Obviously they do not want this situation to change.

Any real socialist government would make sure that such rampant recklessness was no longer allowed. Rules and regulations would be put in place to trammel unfettered and risky investments as well as putting a stop to obscene bonuses. The SNP made no such threats in its White Paper, but who was to say what would happen in the future? Despite what Better Together might say, an independent Scotland would not be a one-party state.

The bankers, therefore, were merely looking after their own interests; and it would not be the first time. All their apparent concerns about unemployment in an independent

Scotland need to be viewed in the context that they are the ones that caused the current economic downturn and the subsequent rise in unemployment. They have not been overly concerned about unemployment in the past, so it is unlikely that they would be concerned about it in the future.

Businesses as well, however, were adamant that there would be major job losses were Scotland to become independent. 130 Scottish business leaders sent an open letter to the Scotsman in August 2014 (even though the heading mistakenly says 'September') ostensibly outlining their concerns. In reality, however, there were no details to be had. Essentially they expected everyone just to take their word for it that things would be bad for business in an independent Scotland. The best they could come up with in the way of explanation was that there was 'uncertainty'.

Uncertainty surrounds a number of vital issues including currency, regulation, tax, pensions, EU membership and support for our exports around the world; and uncertainty is bad for business.[21]

This, of course, was yet another disingenuous argument. Uncertainly also surrounded these 'vital issues' in the United Kingdom, especially the question of EU membership. This was highlighted when 200 other business leaders decided to send their own open letter. Neil Clapperton, managing director of Springbank Distillers, said, 'The biggest threat to the whisky industry comes from the in/out EU referendum the UK is planning, and the fact that this could close EU influence in getting whisky into foreign markets.'[22]

The question of EU membership deserves a chapter of its own but the other worries expressed by the anti-independence business leaders can be dealt with in less detail. The concerns over currency, for example, are easily refuted; more so since no explanation is offered for exactly what it is that concerns these businessmen.

We have already looked at the currency argument and it

came down to an independent Scotland using the Pound in a credit union, the Pound outside a credit union, the Euro or a new currency. No matter which of these options ended up being used, it was hardly going to affect business.

In the unlikely event of Scotland using the Euro this would actually help exports, especially to the remainder of the UK since the Pound has been strong for a while now, and is kept so by the London money markets. The same holds true if Scotland were to have its own currency. The only possible way problems could arise would be if there was to be massive inflation, an unlikely scenario, or if Scotland ended up having a currency that was too strong. If it was the latter case that they were worrying about then it begs the question as to why they are not complaining about the Westminster Government's current obsession with maintaining a strong Pound.

As for regulation, one wonders what regulations they were worried about. Were they afraid of perhaps being forced into paying a living wage? No other regulations regarding business in Scotland had been mooted and it would be a foolhardy government that put obstacles in the way of businesses that provide jobs for its population.

The concerns over tax are rather risible; it is difficult enough at present to get businesses to pay their fair share. No matter what the tax system in an independent Scotland, creative accountants would be on hand to look for loopholes, like companies buying raw materials and services from their own subsidiaries for example. Getting tax out of businesses is like trying to eat tomato soup with a knife and fork; it is as difficult a task as can be imagined. The supposed worry over tax expressed in the open letter, then, is nothing more than nonsense.

The pension worries are just as nonsensical. What are they concerned about; that they will no longer be allowed to steal from pension funds to shore up an ailing business? Again, we do not know since they provide no details.

As well as making trite comments about the dangers of

Scottish independence, the anti-independence business community had another, well-worn card to play. Gavin Hewitt, the former head of the Scotch Whisky Association, 'who helped gather signatories for that letter, said about half the people he had approached were opposed to independence but did not want (to) sign the letter and make their views public for fear of a backlash from the SNP.'[23]

As usual, no evidence whatsoever was provided for these outrageous accusations. There were stories about Sir Peter Housden, the permanent secretary to the Scottish Government, contacting businesses to tell them to keep out of the debate. Some business people made the same kind of allegations about John Swinney, the finance and public services minister. No proof was forthcoming; only the word of 'unnamed sources'.[24]

Meanwhile, it emerged that the CBI had registered as campaigners for a NO vote without the permission of its member companies. In fact, some companies actually pulled out of the CBI in protest.[25] And it also came to light that UK retailers were being urged to spread scare stories about increased prices in an independent Scotland, with the full backing of the Prime Minister.[26] Again, it seemed that the Unionist side was guilty of doing exactly what they were accusing the pro-independence side of.

Of course, there was one UK Government department threatening job losses that was actually telling the truth; the Ministry of Defence. An independent Scotland would no longer provide recruits to the British armed forces, meaning no jobs for soldiers, sailors or air force personnel.

The SNP White Paper had already promised that Scotland would have its own army, navy and air force and had even outlined the funds that would be spent in this area. In fact, it was planned that an independent Scotland would actually spend more on defence in Scotland than the Westminster Government did at present. And, yet, this was still going to be less than Scotland currently contributed to the UK defence budget.[27] Since this planned spending was going to be on conventional forces, rather than on nuclear weapons, it would actually mean more military jobs than there were in a Scotland within the UK.

Laughably, or perhaps tragically, the Henry Jackson Society, another right-wing think-tank, produced a report about defence in an independent Scotland, which suggested that recruitment would be a problem, since armed forces personnel would rather see action than 'twiddle their thumbs' in a Scottish Defence Force. The Daily Mail called the report 'damning'[28] and damning it most certainly was, although not in the way the paper intended. It is, in fact, a damning indictment of the British Army if it is true that young men are joining up, not out of a patriotic desire to defend their country, but out of some psychotic urge to shoot people. Thankfully, only one platoon of thirty-two men was surveyed.[29]

It would be interesting to find out if the report's extrapolation from this one platoon was correct or if the opposite was the case. How many more young people would be willing to carve out a career in the army if there was no longer the threat of being sent to some far-flung place to get shot at or blown up in a war of dubious legality? Unfortunately, the MoD will not allow such surveys since it has to be seen to be politically neutral. This begs the question, of course, as to who commissioned and paid for the 'damning' HJS report.

It is worth noting that the Henry Jackson Society is no stranger to controversy. Its associate director, Douglas Murray, wrote an article in 2013, which would not look out of place on a BNP website. In it he said, 'London has become a foreign country. In 23 of London's 33 boroughs "white Britons" are now in a minority.'[30]

Also worth noting is the fact that the author of the HJS report, George Grant, is standing as a Conservative candidate in the 2015 General Election.[31] So neither the author, nor the organisation to which he belongs, are exactly what you would call neutral observers!

The MoD was also involved in another major wrangle about jobs. In August 2014 the Ministry announced that three Offshore Patrol Vessels for the Royal Navy would be built on the Clyde; a contract worth £348m. There was a catch, however; Michael Fallon, the UK Defence Secretary, said, 'UK warships are only built in UK shipyards.'[32] In other words, if Scotland voted for independence then it could kiss goodbye to this order.

It could also say cheerio to the proposed order for thirteen Type 26 frigates. The plan was that these new warships be built on the Clyde but it was made plain that no contract would be signed until after the referendum and, even then, it would only be finalised if Scotland voted NO. The reason given was that if Scotland became independent it would effectively be a foreign country and the MoD has a policy of only building complex warships within the UK.[33]

Although arguments were made against this stance it seems fair enough on the face of it. After Scotland did actually vote NO, however, there was still a delay in the contracts being signed. The head of the Royal Navy, First Sea Lord Admiral George Zambellas, explained that affordability was the main concern and that a final decision had not yet been made. There was speculation that the frigates might be bought from France, while Zambellas himself said:

The affordability question that comes from that depends on the best that industry can deliver. You'll notice I haven't necessarily said that that's the British industry, as the decision has not been made on what the solution to the requirement will be.'[34]

The Defence Secretary, Michael Fallon, was quick to dismiss such claims and say that the warships would definitely be built on the Clyde.[35] As of January 2015, however, the contracts had still not been signed.

It might well be that the frigates will be built on the Clyde, but the fact remains that a question mark hangs over the whole claim that such warships have to be built within the UK. If the MoD can even consider purchasing such vessels abroad then it obviously gives the lie to the claims that they could not be built in an independent Scotland. Either that or the MoD was going to have to admit that a bumbling oaf was in charge of Britain's Senior Service. On this evidence it would appear that not giving the contract to the Clyde shipyards was simply to be a petulant punishment for voting for independence.

There was some speculation that deals would be made if Scotland were to become independent, including the possibility that keeping Trident on the Clyde would be a bargaining tool.[36] Whether this scenario became a reality, however, was debatable; everyone involved in the independence campaign was adamant that they wanted no nuclear weapons based in Scotland. Of course, this would mean job losses as well.

No matter what anyone's thoughts are on nuclear weapons, or having them deployed so close to Scotland's most populated area, there was no denying that thousands of jobs, and potential jobs depended on Faslane. When you take into account all the other jobs and businesses; shops, schools etc. reliant on the workers at Faslane then the job losses were going to be huge. This was one of the trump cards of Better Together and was a major reason for people choosing to vote NO.

Since there was no arguing this point, the only way that the pro-independence side could counter it was by showing that other jobs would replace these losses. Fortunately, there was already another source of employment possible, and on the same site.

For decades there have been stories circulating of a huge oil find in the Firth of Clyde. MSP Chic Brodie spent over two years investigating these stories; interviewing oil workers, oil companies, MoD officials and their counterparts in the USA. He reached the conclusion that oil had been found but that the discovery had been hidden.[37]

It seems that further investigation in the Clyde was halted by the MoD so as to maintain the area for the training and exercise of nuclear submarines.[38] Rather conveniently, the MoD's records on the exploration have vanished, as have the relevant records at BP. It is the usual practice for the Department of Energy to keep records of such surveys; strangely, however, the department claims to have no such records in this particular case.[39] Both Chic Brodie and retired Labour politician David Lambie suspected a cover-up. And given Denis Healey's assertions regarding the playing down of Scotland's oil reserves in the 1970s and 1980s, there was, and still is, every reason to believe them.

The Sunday Post, while reporting on the story, took the opportunity to quote Aberdeen University's Professor Alex Kemp, whom they described as 'a world leading expert on oil and gas exploration'. Professor Kemp, while admitting that it was probable that the MoD stopped exploration, said, 'I would be surprised if there is anything there.'[40]

Well, that quotation certainly put a damper on things; an expert maintaining that there was no oil or gas under the Firth of Clyde appeared to draw a line under the speculation. Professor Kemp *is* a world-renowned expert in the oil industry and has worked as an adviser to the UK Government.[41] He is, however, an economist, not a seismologist, geologist or mineralogist. No doubt he has picked up a few smatterings of knowledge of oil and gas exploration in his work but this does not make him an expert in the field. Historians necessarily pick up some knowledge of economics in their studies, but none would put themselves forward as an expert in this area. Equally, Professor Kemp should not be viewed as an expert in the area of oil and gas exploration, as the Sunday Post claims. Not surprisingly, the Sunday Post was firmly in the camp of the Unionists.

The whole Better Together and Unionist claim that there would be massive unemployment in an independent

Scotland was based on nothing more than half-truths, concealments and downright lies. At any rate, there was already massive unemployment in Scotland and this was the next point of attack by Better Together: how would an independent Scotland fund welfare payments? This concerned not only the unemployed but the increasing numbers of old-age pensioners as well.

7

Farewell Welfare?

There are areas of Scotland where poverty and deprivation are still everyday parts of people's lives. This is Thatcher's legacy to Scotland; dead-end lives with nothing whatsoever to look forward to. It sounds depressing and it is; in fact, clinical depression is almost a plague in these places, affecting everyone with a fatalistic apathy.

For those of us that grew up in the 1960s and 1970s ambition was a normal part of growing up. Children would aim to get the same jobs as their mothers or fathers, or maybe even be encouraged by their parents to set their sights higher. Nowadays, however, there are many children whose parents, or even grandparents, have never had a job in their lives. To these children ambition is an alien concept and anyone involved in trying to educate them has an almost impossible task on his or her hands.

These folk have become dispossessed and feel totally uninvolved and unrepresented in society; and they are not far wrong in their feelings. And to make things worse, they often find themselves blamed for their debased circumstances. They are constantly harried to find jobs that do not exist and now they are being forced into virtual slavery with the Work Fair scheme.

It is perhaps telling that the attitude of Better Together was not how an independent Scotland would get all these folk into work, but how it would pay for them. This would be especially the case since the SNP had promised to get rid of many of the draconian measures of the Westminster Government, such as the so-called 'bedroom tax'.

There were warnings too from the group set up by Nicola Sturgeon to look into the welfare system in an independent Scotland. The group said that a sudden change would lead to 'serious risk to the continuity of payments', not just in

Scotland but in England and Wales.[1] The panel recommended having a transitional period, with Scotland still part of the UK-wide system until appropriate, separate systems had been implemented.

The Scottish Government took on board these recommendations and made new plans to have this transitional stage should Scotland become independent.[2] These plans, however, would depend on the agreement of Westminster, which had already refused to agree on any shared enterprise after independence, even a temporary one.

And, of course, the Department for Work and Pensions did not disappoint. There was the usual talk about logistic concerns, as well as the fear that Scotland would not be using the Pound. A shared database, it seemed, would be unable to cope with changes that an independent Scottish Government might make to benefits in Scotland. In an official paper, the department said:

Sharing [information technology] systems and services would mean that an independent Scottish state would not be able to make changes to existing social security policy or processes or to opt out of Great Britain wide reforms. Reconfiguring the current system to meet the demands of two governments with different policies would introduce additional costs and risks. This would not be in the interests of the government of the continuing UK.[3]

This is absolute piffle. Even basic databases, like the ones pupils use in primary schools, are remarkably flexible programmes. I taught Primary 5 pupils how to make a database of school library books; the programme itself cross-referenced the data to make it easy to access. One could then type in 'Romans' and find all the books with the word in the title, or input an author's name and see all the books written by that person in the school's possession. Are we supposed to believe that the IT consultants used by Government departments are less capable than nine-year-old children? The truth is that mass changes on a database can be done with the click of a button. Again, Westminster was simply creating obstacles to put in the way of Scottish independence.

It is strange how the Westminster Government seems to only stand up for democracy when it suits it. There is constant diplomatic disagreement with Spain over Gibraltar; the UK Government insisting that it is the democratic wish of the people of Gibraltar to remain British. There was also no compunction in sending troops thousands of miles to uphold the democratic right of the Falkland Islanders to also remain British. And yet every obstacle was being put in the way of the Scottish people exercising its democratic right to leave the UK. It would appear that, to Westminster, remaining British is the main concern, rather than democratic rights!

At any rate, we were told continually that people on benefits were going to suffer if Scotland voted for independence. Iain Duncan Smith, the Westminster Work and Pensions Secretary, said, 'Proposals by the Scottish Government would risk the well-being of vulnerable people who are currently supported by this system.'[4] Would that be the same vulnerable people that the Coalition Government has been forcing back into work, even when they are incapable?

As usual, hypocrisy and lies were the order of the day when it came to the Unionist cause. Gordon Brown also claimed that the vulnerable would be at risk if Scotland voted YES, stating that such a vote 'could leave Scotland a poorer and more unequal country.'[5] That was nothing more than a sick joke at Scotland's expense; it had been an unequal country for decades. Thirteen years of Labour rule at Westminster and eight years at Holyrood had made not one iota of difference.

Brown continued, 'The Scots, English, Welsh and Northern Irish have equal rights to... fully funded healthcare free at the point of need'.[6] We have already seen that such claims were nothing but lies (See Chapter 6) so why should Brown be trusted when it came to the rest of his warnings?

As it turned out, the people that were being targeted with these lies and disinformation did not trust Brown and his fellow Unionists. Early analyses of demographic patterns in the referendum shows that areas of high unemployment tended to vote for independence.[7] With the average voter turnout in Scotland running at over 84%, and reaching over 90% in some areas,[8] it showed that those that normally felt uninvolved in politics were now looking to become a part of the democratic process.

The same analyses showed that the older one got, the more likely one was to have voted NO.[9] Obviously, somebody had been persuaded by the Unionist case. Considering that the whole Unionist case was about instilling fear then Better Together must have succeeded in making older people afraid of what the future might hold in an independent Scotland. Since these older folks stand out as a distinct group that voted NO, there was evidently something particular that made them nervous. That something was the supposed risk to pensions if Scotland was to leave the UK.

To be fair to Westminster, the UK Pensions Minister had said that state pensions would be secure if Scotland were to become independent. He said that Scottish people 'have accumulated rights into the UK system, under the UK system's rules'. He added, 'Citizenship is irrelevant. It is what you have put into the UK National Insurance system prior to separation'.[10] There might be a bit of haggling over who paid what but, essentially, older people had nothing to worry about.

Private pensions with the likes of Scottish Widows or Standard Life would also be safe, as the companies involved had contingency plans in place.[11] There were concerns, however, over company pension schemes since EU regulations said that cross-border schemes had to be 'fully-funded'; essentially a company would have to show that it had enough funds to pay out if such pensions had to be paid now.[12] Apparently many companies would be unable to comply with this rule, as it was not the norm for companies to set aside funds in this way. (I would have thought that this fact was far more worrying than what might happen if Scotland became independent!)

The horror story being peddled by the Unionists was that an independent Scotland would be unable to provide for its pensioners in the future. Figures provided by the UK Treasury said that there were currently 28.5 people over the age of 65 to every 100 workers. By 2060 this was expected to be 45.9 people of pension age to every 100 workers. These were figures for the whole of the UK; Scotland's pensioners were expected to increase to 51.7 to every 100 workers by the same date.[13] How would Scotland pay for this aging population if it became independent?

2060 is a long way off and anything could change in that near half-century, both in the UK and in Scotland, independent or not. To read the headlines of the Unionist press, however, one would think that the population was going to suddenly age overnight. Either that or they wanted all the current pensioners to believe that their pensions were at risk. Many folk only look at the headlines and the papers made sure that their headlines did not fully reflect the content of the articles they headed.

Scottish independence vote could prompt pensions crisis.[14]

Scottish independence: Yes vote 'threat to pensions'.[15]

Pensions meltdown fear if Scots vote for split.[16]

Pension fears raised ahead of referendum.[17]

Any pensioner reading one of those headlines would have serious concerns about where their next Werther's Original was going to come from! And, of course, Better Together made sure that the point was pressed home. Gordon Brown, for example, banged on about how Scottish pensioners received more than those in the rest of the UK, when you took into account winter fuel allowances and the like. They would lose out on all this if they voted for independence.[18] Since Westminster had already guaranteed that pensioners had nothing to worry about then Brown's warnings were nothing more than a cynical pack of lies!

Jim Murphy, meanwhile, spoke of the disruption that would ensue with independence, affecting everyone's wallet in the process. More devolved powers would be better, including looking at 'how we can decentralise aspects of the social security system.'[19] But was that not going to cost hundreds of millions of pounds to set up? That is what they were telling us would happen if the system was decentralised due to Scottish independence. How would it be any different in Murphy's scenario? Again, we were being fed nothing but disinformation by Better Together.

It was clear that Murphy had no real understanding of the issues involved in the referendum; like others in the Better Together campaign, he saw it as merely the nationalists promising people more money, while blaming the English for all the current problems in Scotland. His dogged adherence to these beliefs became clear in January 2015, well after the referendum was over.

The so-called Mansion Tax has been bandied about by Labour for the past couple of years and, on the face of it, seems a reasonable enough way to redistribute some of the wealth in the UK. The noises coming from Labour seem to be that the money raised will be spent on the NHS. Under the Barnett Formula Scotland's grant would be increased due to this extra spending to the tune of about £250million. It seemed fair enough; but, then, along came Jim Murphy.

Murphy announced that, should Labour be in power in both Westminster and Holyrood then this windfall would be used to pay for an extra 1000 nurses.[20] Cue outrage from London, where by far the largest portion of the tax will be levied. Both Boris Johnson, the current mayor, and Diane Abbott, a Labour candidate for the post, were dead against the whole idea; especially in the way Jim Murphy was describing it.[21]

The obvious, knee-jerk reaction is to have no sympathy for London millionaires, whose numbers include Boris Johnson himself. What happened to all the rhetoric about being 'one nation' and 'pooling resources'? Evidently, Londoners are happy enough when taxes, including those from oil and gas, flow from Scotland to the capital but are up in arms when it is the other way about! Johnson, however, does have a point when he calls this plan of Murphy's nothing more than a 'bribe' to Scottish voters.[22]

If anything, Murphy's envisaged plan shows remarkable contempt for the Scottish electorate, especially those that supported independence. Scottish Labour is toeing the UK party line that the fight for independence was about nothing more than looking for more money and anti-English racism. To pander to these perceived elements, Scottish Labour is offering a 'Double Whammy' of more cash spent on the NHS in Scotland, which will be grabbed from the supposedly hated English! It shows a remarkable lack of understanding as well as a rather sinister degree of cynicism.

Back to the pensioners in the referendum and it was fairly obvious that the Better Together campaign of fear was paying dividends. An opinion poll on the run-up to the vote showed that nearly three-quarters of Scottish pensioners were worried about their pensions if there was a YES vote.[23] So, despite the fact that both Holyrood and Westminster had promised that pensions would be protected, Scottish OAPs were being led to believe that their pensions were at risk. Essentially, they were being lied to.

And so, one group, Scotland's pensioners and those coming up to pension age, were taken in by the lies of Better Together, while another, those living in poverty and deprivation, was not. As stated earlier, it could be argued that those in deprived areas had nothing to lose by voting YES; this, however, does not tell the whole story.

The general image of the unemployed throughout the UK is one of shiftless, work-shy scoundrels, like the Gallagher family in the TV programme 'Shameless'. Scotland is often portrayed as living under a 'benefit culture' and those on unemployment or sickness benefits are viewed as being unwilling to work and perfectly happy to 'sponge' off the state. The independence referendum proved that this image was entirely false.

Better Together did not just claim that pensions would be under threat in an independent Scotland; all welfare payments were at risk. With that in mind, then, it would appear that those on benefits, like Scottish pensioners, actually had everything to lose. And yet, the majority of this group voted YES. What was independence offering that tempted them?

In order to pay for an aging population in the future, an independent Scotland was going to need a bigger workforce. Increased immigration was one answer to this problem[24] but it was obvious that Scotland would not be able to afford the extra burden of a large proportion of its people being on unemployment benefits as well. These folk were going to have to work; something that, if we believe the stereotypes, should have frightened them to death. Instead, they actually voted to be involved in such a scenario.

Promises were made that an independent Scotland would raise the minimum wage so that it was in line with inflation as well as ensuring that everyone had rights while in employment.[25] So, in effect, those living on benefits in Scotland were voting to get themselves out of the poverty trap and into employment; real employment. They were voting to get back their self-respect, something that Better Together and the Labour Party did not appear to understand.

Sir Harry Burns, who, until quite recently, was Scotland's Chief Medical Officer, used the statistics available, as well as the evidence of his own eyes, to suggest that the referendum vote showed the serious class divisions in Scotland. He said, 'The comfortable middle class voted to stay comfortable. So, who now speaks for the poor? When you think about it, the poor spoke for themselves by voting in huge numbers. They were put back in their place.'[26]

Scottish Labour, of course, was quick to condemn him. One Labour spokesperson said, 'We believe we can achieve equality and social justice by using the opportunity of devolution and the strength of the UK.' He or she also claimed that the referendum vote had not been a class issue, stating that 'Many people from different backgrounds and circumstances voted in the referendum for different reasons'[27]

This ignores all the evidence right under their noses. The fact is that in regions where there were areas of high unemployment and deprivation either YES won or NO won by a very small margin. In places with large concentrations of middle-class voters, like Edinburgh, Stirling, East Renfrewshire and East Dunbartonshire NO won quite comfortably.[28] There was an obvious, glaring pattern that it was impossible to dismiss; Labour, however, was doing just that.

The Labour response to Sir Harry Burns showed a remarkable degree of insensitivity to say the least. They were not listening to the voters, but telling them, patronisingly, what was best for them. This goes a long way to explaining why Labour's core vote had deserted the party. Many of them had given up voting in elections at all but they had turned out in droves to support Scottish independence. Labour should have been learning from this but obviously they were not. It was going to be interesting to see how much this cost Scottish Labour in the way of votes in the 2015 General Election.

But the Better Together depiction of an independent Scotland as a wasteland of unemployment and starving pensioners did not end there. We have already touched on the claims that an independent Scotland would not be allowed into the European Union, with devastating effects on the economy. It is time to look at these claims in more detail.

8
Euro Furore

A major part of the pro-independence campaign was that Scotland would still be part of the European Union. The theory was that Scotland already had six MEPs so it would be a relatively simple matter to transfer its membership from being a part of the UK to being an independent nation. There were arguments, however, that things might not be so cut-and-dried.

Much was made of new EU President, Jean-Claude Juncker, declaring a moratorium on new admissions to the European Union. He said that it was time to consolidate the achievements so far and placed a five-year freeze on any new nations being admitted. According to Better Together this dashed any hopes that an independent Scotland would be automatically accepted as members of the EU.[1] That, however, was not the end of the matter.

No sooner had the Unionists started gloating over Juncker's decision than a hurried explanation was forthcoming from the President's staff that he had not, in fact, been talking about Scotland.[2] Of course, Better Together did not see this as a setback and continued to claim that EU membership would not be transferred to an independent Scotland.

These arguments were, as usual filled with 'ifs', 'buts' and 'maybes', as well as the half-truths we came to expect. Fears were raised that Spain would veto Scotland's membership since it would set a precedent for Catalan and Basque aspirations.[3] There were also noises made about the Flemish seceding from Belgium, Corsica from France and even Hungarian Transylvanians seeking autonomy from Romania. It looked like there would be a whole range of nations ready to stand in Scotland's way if it wanted to be in the EU.

This was something that used to trouble me when I was studying History, 'Germany wanted to…', 'France thought…' etc. as if a whole nation of millions of souls was of one mind. You hear this stuff all the time; for example, the papers will tell you how cruel Spain is, still having bull fighting. In Spain, however, there are animals' rights groups, just like in this country, who campaign to have bull fighting stopped. The Corridas themselves, meanwhile, are sparsely attended; many people in Spain find them an anachronism and an irrelevance. In fact, it is probably only the tourists that keep the things going.

It is the same with other matters in Spain; not everybody feels the same way. People from Castile can be quite snooty and I am sure that there are many of them that would like to get rid of the Basques and the Catalans, much like a lot of English folk would love to see the back of the Scots! At any rate, not everybody in Spain would be upset at Scotland becoming independent; there are no doubt many Spaniards that would, perhaps, relish inviting a breakaway nation into the EU, hoping for support when it comes to Gibraltar.

It is notable that, for all the Unionist rhetoric about what Spain, Belgium and the rest were going to do, nobody actually bothered to question anyone from the nations concerned. It was not until after the referendum was over that the BBC decided to address this issue properly.

In an article telling us how relieved nations were that Scotland had voted NO, different writers reported on different countries so that we could see the full impact of the referendum outcome.[4] The article made for very interesting reading.

SPAIN: 'Catalans who passionately want Catalonia to remain part of Spain say the situation here is more complicated than, in the words of one activist, a "black-and-white, yes-no" decision.'

CANADA: 'Quebec's Premier Philippe Couillard said that while Scotland's referendum was an example of the same kind of healthy tension that exists in Quebec, all comparisons after that were "risky".'

INDIA: 'India's foreign minister didn't know Scotland was considering divorce, until an aide whispered in her ear.'

ROMANIA: 'The Democratic Union of Hungarians (UDMR), who form part of the current Romanian government, this week published their own plans for Szekler autonomy, based on the model of Italy's South Tyrol province. Leader Hunor Kelemen stressed the difference between the plan and Scotland's referendum.'

It seemed, therefore, that things were not as cut-and-dried as the Unionists were making out. There were not nations throughout Europe and the world desperate for Scotland to vote NO. Another commentator put it even more explicitly. '...political scientists have found that separatism in one country doesn't necessarily promote separatism in another, said Jason Sorens, a government professor at Dartmouth College.'[5] So the Unionists were merely peddling their usual tales of fear.

It has to be said that there were those in Europe that were relieved that Scotland had voted NO; among them Angela Merkel, the German Chancellor. Why? With Scotland still part of the UK there is less chance of it leaving the EU.[6] This turns the whole separatist argument on its head; it was UK separatists that were worrying German politicians, not Scottish ones!

Notice that I said 'German politicians' and not 'Germany'; there were probably plenty of Germans that would be more than happy at seeing the break-up of the UK. The fact is that the UK is not as popular in Europe as many folk here like to think. The close relationship between Britain and the USA caused Charles De Gaulle to continually fight against the UK becoming part of the Common Market and there are still many that dislike and distrust Britain. One only has to witness the 'nul points' frequently doled out to the UK in the Eurovision Song Contest for proof!

There was no way of predicting, then, what the response would be to an independent Scotland being part of the EU; but that did not stop the Unionist media and Better Together attempting to do so. The fact that they provided no evidence from the countries concerned but merely the opinions of 'experts', however, showed that there was no real substance to their claims.

They also pointed to the fact that new nations joining the EU were required to use the Euro as their currency.[7] This, however, depended on the assumption that Scotland would, in fact, be treated as a new member nation. Scotland already has six representatives in the EU and has been adhering to European law for decades now; the possibility was that Scotland would not be seen as a new member.

There is actually a precedent for an independent Scotland to be seen as a continuing member of the EU, though at first sight it might not seem so. In 1990 East and West Germany were reunited to create the new nation of Germany. When it came to membership of the European Community, as it was then, there was no need for this new nation to apply; it was assumed that the new Germany was simply a continuation of the Federal Republic of Germany (West Germany), inheriting the Federal Republic's membership.[8] Surely a case could be made for an independent Scotland to inherit its share of the UK's membership in precisely the same way?

It seemed, though, that some kind of compromise solution might be possible, or, indeed, probable. While the EU debated on Scotland's position in Brussels it was likely that some kind of interim arrangement would be put in place where Scotland would be members in all but name.[9]

Whatever the truth was about how an independent Scotland would be treated by the EU there was another prospect to consider, one we have already encountered: the withdrawal of the UK from Europe. This was a distinct possibility and something that Better Together and its allies in the media attempted at all costs to ignore or play down. While broadcasting scare stories of an independent Scotland being stuck outside the EU, they neglected to mention that a NO vote could well present the same scenario.

In July 2014, as we saw earlier, David Cameron filled his cabinet with Eurosceptics. (See Chapter 2) This was in response to the upsurge in support for the UK Independence Party, UKIP, in England. Many Tories have long been calling for a referendum on Europe, determined that the UK should leave. Recently, not only Tory voters but Tory MPs have defected to UKIP, making it seem all the more likely that Britain will leave the EU. Cameron has already promised that the long-desired referendum will take place after the next general election.[10]

To be fair, many of the same businessmen and politicians that argued for Scotland to remain in the UK are also dead against Britain leaving the EU.[11] They are not happy about certain aspects of the EU, such as their employees actually having rights, but they realise that it would be an extremely bad idea to leave altogether. In fact, they are not overly chuffed even with the idea of a referendum, feeling that it will lead to uncertainty when it comes to other countries trading with the UK.[12]

These were the same arguments we heard about Scotland leaving the UK and even about the referendum itself. We were forever hearing how businesses were holding off investing or hiring employees until the uncertainty was over. This was all the fault, of course, of Alex Salmond and the SNP for calling the referendum in the first place. They were gambling with Scotland's future just for some old-fashioned sense of nationalism.

Looking back at the Better Together campaign, the whole argument that they presented was solely based on economics and business concerns. When YES campaigners tried to discuss welfare all the NO side could contend with was scare stories about funding and taxation. One commentator suggested that they had no alternative, since 'British Nationalism' had so many pejorative connotations.[13] Blair McDougall, head of the Better Together campaign, admitted after the referendum that it was their negative, economic scare stories that actually won them the vote.[14]

As we have already seen, top businessmen, bankers and economists were wheeled out to argue that leaving the UK was a mistake. Better Together constantly quoted these experts to show that nothing else mattered in the referendum except the economy and business. There was even some anger that a referendum had even been set in motion in the first place. It was to be expected that the same arguments would be to the forefront when it came to a referendum on the UK leaving Europe.

With all the vaunted economic uncertainty that had supposedly occurred due to the Scottish independence referendum, one would expect that the Westminster Government would be rather reluctant to countenance a referendum on EU membership. The CBI's warnings in this respect should act as a fillip to any such reluctance; after all, as we were constantly told during the 2014 referendum, business and the economy are paramount. And yet, David Cameron is adamant that, should the Conservatives win the 2015 General Election, such a referendum will go ahead.

Although Euroscepticism has long been part-and-parcel of right-wing Conservatism, it is really the rise of UKIP that has inspired this urgent desire for a referendum on Europe. In effect, UKIP is determining the whole essence of the debate on membership of the EU and that debate is not based on business concerns; in fact, it is rather anti-business in its arguments.

Ever since the Industrial Revolution businessmen have looked to cut costs and maximise profits by importing workers that they can pay less and exploit more than the local population. Throughout the UK poverty-stricken refugees from the countryside, the Scottish Highlands, Ireland, the West Indies and the Indian subcontinent were successively used in this way. This has become one of the mainstays of British business and is still going on with the importation of workers from Eastern Europe.

At each stage of these successive immigrations the local population has acquiesced only reluctantly to having strangers in its midst. In times of high unemployment, however, tensions can boil over into xenophobic and racist hatred. This happened in the 1930s and 1970s and is happening again now with the rise of UKIP.

A look at the UKIP website gives a true picture of what its concerns are; immigrants stealing British jobs, foreign cultures invading Britain and nasty Muslims frightening the kiddies by having their faces covered.[15] (Looking at some of the pictures on the website perhaps the covering of faces is a practice that should be adopted by more people, Muslim or not!) Nothing at all is said about business or the economy; that is way down the list of priorities.

Ensuring that immigration is cut and that immigrants are kept out of jobs that are reserved for British workers will necessarily drive wages up as the workforce pool becomes smaller. Businesses will not be happy about this and will pull out of the UK in droves. Is this not what we were being warned about during the Scottish independence referendum campaign? At any rate, UKIP does not seem to be overly concerned about it.

The rise of UKIP as a political force has taken almost everyone by surprise. It was always a party that stood at the fringes, a laughing-stock that attracted politicians manqués, like Robert Kilroy-Silk. Now it is challenging the main UK political parties all over England. And Scotland has not escaped either; it currently has a UKIP MEP. It seems that the xenophobia and racism of working-class Britain was completely underestimated.

While UKIP denies being the BNP in a suit and tie, that has not stopped them from forging alliances with right-wing extremists in Brussels.[16] Meanwhile stories keep emerging of the racist and fascist beliefs of many in the party itself. None of this, however, has diminished its support, which only goes to show what the appeal of the party actually is.

And so, if the Conservatives win the next election, or end up in some kind of partnership with UKIP to form a government, we are going to be subjected to a referendum that most business leaders do not want. We were told constantly throughout the Scottish independence referendum

117

campaign that business and the economy were the most important elements to be considered. It seems, however, that other considerations are more important when it comes to this other referendum.

The arguments about Europe, then, showed up the falsehoods inherent in the Better Together campaign. Not only were they lying about business being the most important consideration, when they knew that this would not be the case in the referendum on Europe, but they were also less than truthful about Scotland remaining part of the EU. It might involve an interim period of not being a full member but it was clear that there would be no problem with an independent Scotland staying in the European Union. As part of the UK, on the other hand, Scotland might well end up on the outside looking in.

Of course, as well as appealing to its core demographic, UKIP has to try and get others onside if it stands any chance of increased success electorally. To this end it has come up with a madcap plan to replace Britain's trade links in Europe with some sort of Zollverein within the Commonwealth. This assumes that the Commonwealth nations are all desperately awaiting the return of 'Bwana' to rescue them from their current trade problems. It also begs the question of why Britain joined the Common Market in the first place if everything was previously so rosy!

At any rate, speaking of the Commonwealth leads on to the next mendacious part of the Better Together campaign: the monarchy. Apparently, unlike every other Commonwealth nation, there were going to be major problems with the Queen being head of state in an independent Scotland.

9

Queen of Scots

Many people in the UK see the monarchy as an expensive anachronism and an irrelevance. Monarchs no longer lead troops into battle and the days when we believed that they were God's chosen and could heal the sick are long gone. Arguments that they are necessary for tourism and trade do not hold water; other nations, the USA for example, seem to manage fine without kings or queens.

Nevertheless, there are still people that desperately want to hold onto the monarchy, for whatever reasons. Any debate on the matter usually degenerates into aggressive abuse from the royalist side. It does not matter what kind of logical arguments one puts forward; they will not yield an inch.

The Unionist side preyed on the fears of such people, saying that the monarchy would be under threat if Scotland were to become independent.[1] Some commentators concentrated on the fact that Alex Salmond was once part of a republican group[2] while others suggested that the Queen would abdicate rather than suffer the loss of part of her kingdom.[3] No matter how they worded it the implication was always there: vote YES and lose the Queen.

Alex Salmond's republican past was brought up to show that he could not be trusted when it came to the monarchy.[4] This, however, could easily be explained as political compromise, a tactic that all parties employ in order to get elected. It hardly proved that there was the probability of abolishing the monarchy in an independent Scotland; but, still, the media persisted in pushing the argument. The truth is, however, that it was all nonsense.

When Queen Elizabeth I of England died in 1603 she was the last of the Tudor line. The next in line to the throne would have been Mary Queen of Scots, if she had bided her time and not got involved in silly plots. As it was, her son, James VI, became James I of England; and so began the Stuart dynasty.

When James VII and II was deposed, his Protestant daughter Mary took the throne jointly with her husband, William of Orange. This pair died childless so Mary's sister Anne, who had also been raised a Protestant, became queen. Queen Anne tragically lost seventeen children, who were either still-born or died in childhood. And so the Stuart dynasty, like the Tudor before it, came to an end. There were still Stuarts extant but they were Catholics and ineligible to sit on either the throne of Scotland or England.

The Act of Settlement of 1701 had established that no Catholic, or anyone married to a Catholic, could become monarch of England, as well as strengthening the Bill of Rights to limit the powers of the monarchy.[5] Queen Mary had died childless and it looked like Queen Anne was going to suffer a similar fate, so family trees had to be scrutinised to find a suitable, Protestant heir.

In 1613 Princess Elizabeth, daughter of James VI and I, married Frederick V, Count Palatine of the Rhine.[6] They were apparently very much in love and proved it by having 13 children. By 1701, however, when the Act of Settlement was drawn up, only two of these children were still alive; Sophia, Electress of Hanover and her elder sister, Louise Hollandine.[7] The latter by this time had become a Catholic and a Cistercian nun, automatically disqualifying her from the succession.[8] Of course, some of Sophia's elder siblings had children of their own but these were either already dead, married to Catholics or of dubious legitimacy. Sophia was the only option.

Sophia lived to the ripe old age of 83 but died just two months before Queen Anne so she never ascended the new, joint throne of the United Kingdom. The succession passed to her son, George Louis, who became George I of

Great Britain and Ireland in 1714. He owed his throne to his Stuart ancestry, which essentially meant that although he was king of the United Kingdom, he was king of Scotland first and foremost.

The current Queen is a direct descendant of George I and so, ultimately, claims her throne, as he did, through her antecedents in the Stuart family. So, just like him, she is monarch of Scotland first, monarch of England second.

In 1977, her Silver Jubilee year, the Queen said the following to both Houses of Parliament:

But I cannot forget that I was crowned Queen of the United Kingdom of Great Britain and Northern Ireland. Perhaps this Jubilee is a time to remind ourselves of the benefits which union has conferred, at home and in our international dealings, on the inhabitants of all parts of this United Kingdom.[9]

To the Unionists this was not only proof positive of where the Queen stood on the issue of Scottish independence, but also a pointer to the fact that she was queen of a united kingdom, not separate nations.

Certainly, when the Queen took the coronation oath, she had to answer in the affirmative the following question:

Will you solemnly promise and swear to govern the Peoples of the United Kingdom of Great Britain and Northern Ireland, Canada, Australia, New Zealand, the Union of South Africa, Pakistan, and Ceylon, and of your Possessions and the other Territories to any of them belonging or pertaining, according to their respective laws and customs?[10]

There are, however, a couple of points worth noting about this oath.

The first is the phrase 'according to their respective laws and customs'. Preceding this is a list of the territories (or, at least, some of them) where the Queen is Head of State. The odd thing is that the United Kingdom is listed as one of the nations where she is going to govern it 'according' to its 'laws and customs'. The glaring anomaly here is that the United Kingdom does not, in fact, have one set of laws and customs. Scotland and England both have completely separate laws; as does Northern Ireland, for that matter.

Furthermore, she promised to govern the *peoples* 'of the United Kingdom of Great Britain and Northern Ireland…according to their respective laws and customs.' This gives the whole oath a completely different meaning; one that would not be to the liking of the Unionist side. From this perspective it can be said that the Queen has promised to govern the *different* peoples of the United Kingdom according to their *different* laws and customs. In that case, if Scotland were to vote to become independent that would become the law of that particular part of the United Kingdom, something which the Queen has promised to uphold.

Another point worth noting is the next part of the Coronation Oath, where the Queen was asked:

Will you maintain and preserve inviolably the settlement of the Church of England, and the doctrine, worship, discipline, and government thereof, as by law established in England? And will you preserve unto the Bishops and Clergy of England, and to the Churches there committed to their charge, all such rights and privileges, as by law do or shall appertain to them or any of them?[11]

There is nothing there about United Kingdoms and the rest; it is purely an oath as the Queen of England. The Queen also took an oath to preserve the Church of Scotland but this was done separately, well before the Coronation, in a meeting with the Privy Council immediately she acceded to the throne.[12]

There is already precedent, therefore, for a British monarch to make separate oaths concerning different parts of the United Kingdom; important oaths too since the whole concept of royalty is wrapped up in religion. So what is to stop a future monarch from taking separate oaths to be King or Queen of Scotland and King or Queen of the remainder of the United Kingdom?

It would not be the first time that the Coronation Oath was changed. In 1953 the present queen, unlike her father, grandfather and great-grandfather, was not declared Emperor of India,[13] since it had become independent in 1947. If Canada, Australia or New Zealand were to decide to become republics sometime in the future, then the wording would have to be changed again.

Another, more fundamental, change took place at George V's Coronation in 1911. There were virulently anti-Catholic elements to the Oath, to which Edward VII had objected and which George V adamantly refused to include. These parts were about denying transubstantiation in Communion and accusing the Catholic Church of superstition and idolatry. To George V all the Roman Catholics in Britain were his subjects as much as the Protestants and he had no desire to cause them any upset.[14] Finally, the offending parts were removed and no longer form a part of the Coronation Oath.

Any claims, then, that the Coronation Oath is ancient, traditional and inviolate are false; it has been tweaked before to meet changing circumstances. There was nothing whatsoever to stop it being slightly altered again to accommodate Scotland becoming independent.

The Queen, by descent and through her Coronation Oath, then, is de facto Queen of Scotland. Future Coronation Oaths might have to be changed slightly but, as it stands, Queen Elizabeth is the monarch of Scotland. When the Scottish Parliament dissolved itself in 1707 there was no abolition of the monarchy. Queen Ann was monarch of Scotland as well as England and all that was changed was the nomenclature: Queen of the United Kingdom instead of two, separate nations. It would be an easy matter to change the nomenclature back.

Of course, at some future date in an independent Scotland the monarchy might be abolished; but, then, the same could be said for the United Kingdom. There are plenty of republicans in England and Wales so there is nothing peculiarly risky to the monarchy in an independent Scotland. As in the UK, the abolition of the monarchy in an independent Scotland would probably require the support of a majority vote in a referendum. But who is to say what might happen in the future?

As it is, Scottish independence would not affect the Queen's standing as monarch of Scotland. Any suggestion otherwise was a lie and just another scare story from Better Together!

The Queen herself played the neutral observer; officially at any rate. At the start of September 2014, however, there were calls from senior MPs from both sides of the House for David Cameron to persuade the Queen to speak out in favour of the Union.[15] This was occasioned by the fact that the YES vote had closed the gap in the polls and had even overtaken in some of them. The Unionists began to get desperate.

Dragging the Queen into things, however, was beyond the pale as far as many other politicians and experts were concerned.[16] It seemed the Queen was of the same opinion. A spokesman said:

The sovereign's constitutional impartiality is an established principle of our democracy and one which the Queen has demonstrated throughout her reign. As such, the monarch is above politics, and those in political office have a duty to ensure that this remains the case. Any suggestion that the Queen would wish to influence the outcome of the current referendum campaign is categorically wrong. Her Majesty is firmly of the view that this is a matter for the people of Scotland.[17]

Well, that settled that, then! Except, of course, that it did not. It was only a few days before the vote was to take place that it was reported that the Queen had actually come out and commented on the referendum. While leaving Crathie Kirk, near the Balmoral Estate, she took a slight detour to speak to the small crowd that, as usual, was standing about, waiting to get a glimpse of her. She said to the people in the crowd, when someone mentioned the referendum, 'Well, I hope people will think very carefully about the future.'[18]

Those on the Unionist side immediately pounced on these words as showing that the Queen was in favour of the status quo.[19] Given her previous pronouncements about preserving the Union, albeit thirty-seven years ago, and the frequent stories in the press about how worried she was, this view was probably correct. Official palace spokespeople tried to play things down but the damage was done; but obviously nobody could have foreseen the Queen making a spontaneous, off-the-cuff remark, could they?

But was the Queen's statement as spontaneous as it seemed? As well as the crowd of royal watchers outside Crathie Kirk that day there were also members of the press a short distance away. In a highly unusual turn of events, a police sergeant invited the press people to witness Her Majesty interacting with the crowd.[20] Normally the Queen would just get into her car and, if the onlookers were lucky, wave out the window as she passed. The fact that she chose that day of all days to speak to the crowd, as well as the press folk being invited to attend, shows that the whole thing was planned. Whatever her official spokespeople might argue, the Queen seemed determined to have her say and the press were to be on hand to witness it.

After the referendum was over David Cameron was overheard, and captured on camera, saying to former New York mayor Michael Bloomberg, 'The definition of relief is being the prime minister of the United Kingdom and ringing the Queen and saying: "It's alright, it's OK". That was something. She purred down the line.'[21] This unwitting gaffe by Cameron betrayed the truth of what many suspected all along: the Queen had been rooting for a NO vote. Her statement outside Crathie Kirk, then, was obviously intended, as many on the Unionist side had claimed, to show support for the anti-independence campaign. So much for being neutral!

Many might claim that the monarchy no longer has the influence it once had and that most voters in Scotland would not be swayed by the Queen's opinion; this, however, is not strictly true. Polls still put support for the monarchy at between 70% and 80%[22] so obviously the Royal Family is still extremely popular; which explains why the SNP abandoned any republican ideas they had. With such massive support evident it goes without saying that many people will be influenced by what the Queen says. Her comment at Crathie probably swayed a lot of undecided voters over to the anti-independence side.

There is also the matter of the Queen being ostensibly apolitical. Nowadays everyone finds it hard to believe a word that comes out of any politician's mouth, but the Queen is above all the petty, partisan politicking, is she not? If she comes down in favour, or against, some proposition then she is obviously speaking out for the good of the nation. And if our apolitical head of state says that one option is better than another, then who are we to disagree?

It is debatable how much influence the Queen's stage-managed performance had but that is not really the point. What is the point is that our supposedly neutral head of state actually came out and supported one side in the referendum campaign. It was an unprecedented, and rather disgraceful, turn of events and made one wonder who was behind it.

We had to wait until December, three months after the vote, to find out the sordid details. It transpired that the Queen did, indeed, want to get involved on the Unionist side but she had to be very careful to still appear to be neutral. Her own private secretary and the cabinet secretary, Britain's top civil servant, put their heads together and came up with the charade that was played out outside Crathie Kirk.[23]

This tawdry little episode does not reflect very well on the Queen at all and casts doubt over the whole idea of the monarch as an impartial head of state; she most manifestly is not. She had got herself involved in one of the Unionists' nefarious schemes and had even plotted to hoodwink her own subjects. All-in-all it has probably been one of the most unedifying chapters in the history of the Royal Family of the United Kingdom.

And, staying with history, the Unionists had another trick up their sleeves; another slur to throw at the independence movement in general and the SNP in particular. It was claimed that Alex Salmond and his party were trying to rewrite history to suit their own agenda..

10
Historical Hysterics

In 2012 the right-wing press was up in arms about the SNP 'rewriting history'. Apparently the new National History 5, which replaces Standard Grade in the Curriculum for Excellence, was going to be missing out the 'Battle of Britain' from the course.[1] Cue outrage from 'concerned' citizens, including one, anonymous teacher, who said that pupils should be learning how 'Britain stood alone for 12 months after Nazi Germany had conquered most of Europe.' Obviously this teacher does not see the irony in this statement; Britain did not stand alone. The pilots in the 'Battle of Britain' were made up of all different nationalities from the Empire and occupied Europe. This was subsequently rewritten to make it seem as if all the pilots involved were solid, upper-class, English chaps. Even the pilots from a working background; from circuses, crop-spraying companies etc. were written out of the narrative. So, effectively, they were moaning at a lie being left out of the History course!

The fact is that it is impossible to teach everything in a History course. For years Her Majesty's Inspectorate has been complaining about a lack of emphasis on Scotland in schools; not just in History, but in other subjects as well. And so the subject has been revamped. Since there is a time limit on how much the pupils can learn, some topics obviously have to make way for this new emphasis on Scotland and its role in the world. From what it says in the Express it looks as if there is still plenty of balance in the course topics.

The Daily Mail wheeled out TV historian Bettany Hughes, who shows a remarkable lack of understanding of the subject by saying, 'It is very dangerous to cherry-pick moments in history.'[2] Does she suggest that pupils learn the whole history of the human race while at school? Obviously I am being facetious here, but History always involves 'cherry-picked moments' that are looked at in detail to put flesh on the bones of an overarching narrative.

Anybody that did Ordinary Grade History back in the day will remember the topic of Britain after 1815, where we looked at the 1832 Reform Act, the 1833 Factory Acts, Chartism and the Anti-Corn Law League, among other things. (Of course, you learned all this stuff and then were asked in the exam to do something stupid like, 'Pretend you are giving a speech at an Anti-Corn Law League meeting…' It really annoyed the hell out of me and it is not surprising that I only scraped a 'C'!) All the teaching was divided into topics, which is exactly how the teaching of the new course is set out. (Hopefully, though, the pupils will be asked real History questions in the exam!)

One thing that did stick out when we did Ordinary Grade History, however, and that was that it was *English* History rather than *British*. I never learned that Chartism was a major force in Scotland until I went to university, or that many middle-class folk in Scotland were involved in the Anti-Corn Law League and the Free Trade movement. How much more engaged might a pupil at St. Roch's Secondary in Glasgow have been if he or she discovered that nearby old streets that used to be in Royston (Garngad), like Cobden Street and Bright Street, were named after leading lights in the Anti-Corn Law League? Or what about pupils in Paisley finding out about Patrick Brewster, minister of Paisley Abbey, who was a major figure in Chartism? It certainly makes a case for looking at topics from a Scottish perspective. And after all; is Scotland not supposed to be part of Britain?

An SQA spokesperson put the matter straight: the History course was split into three components –

Scottish history, British history and European and World history. He said:

World War Two is covered in the European and World History Unit at National 5 level. The content of this Unit reflects a European and World perspective. The course assessment for National 5 History includes an assignment which allows learners the freedom to choose an area of study of interest to them. This would give them the opportunity to study the Battle of Britain or any other historical topic.[3]

If the Second World War was included in the British history component then another topic would have to make way for it. This would no doubt have folk up in arms about something else being omitted!

One fact that both these newspapers failed to mention was that the Curriculum for Excellence was an initiative begun back when Labour was in power in Holyrood. It was Jack McConnell's baby, not Alex Salmond's. Another point they omitted was that the Scottish Association of Teachers of History, whom The Mail quoted as being upset about the changes,[4] was actually involved in drawing up this new curriculum!

The SNP was not involved at all in developing the Curriculum for Excellence so all this stuff in the press was nothing but a pack of lies. Of course, that did not stop the Unionists, and their friends in the media, continue to claim that the SNP was trying to rewrite history; not just in the schools but in its dealings with the electorate.

In June 2013 there was more uproar when Visit Scotland started a timeline on its website, giving important dates in Scottish history. There were ten dates listed; every one of them had to do with the SNP, directly or indirectly. Unionist politicians leapt on it immediately. Scottish Liberal Democrat leader, Willie Rennie, said, 'After being caught red-handed trying to rewrite Scotland's history, is this the kind of Scotland we might expect after independence?'[5] Others bemoaned the inclusion of the first SNP MP being elected in 1945 while the end of WWII was not mentioned.[6] Scottish Labour's Patricia Ferguson asked 'why was this SNP propaganda allowed to exist on a public body's website?'[7]

It certainly looked suspicious, although one wag could not help pointing out in the Telegraph comments section, 'I doubt if anybody is thinking, "1945, the war, did we win or lose that?"'[8] In other words, there were plenty of places where one could find out about British history; Visit Scotland was specifically concerned with Scotland. Still, Scotland was about more than the SNP!

I contacted Visit Scotland myself and a spokesperson told me the following:

The core purpose of our website www.visitscotland.com, is to include useful information on what to see and do and where to stay for people looking to visit Scotland.

The content of the timeline in question was created using research from various external sources. Some key points in Scottish history were within the timeline and included reference to political landmarks - from the formation of the Labour Party in 1888 to the first SNP MP in 1945. It was designed to give a taste of Scottish history and was by no means exhaustive.

The very nature of digital media allowed us to be flexible and we were happy to add in the suggestions received.

Well, that clears things up, eh? As usual, a public body has to tread a fine line so, they cannot say anything that might offend the politicians that had been complaining. Anything that completely contradicted these politicians would be tantamount to calling them liars and that could end up with the body concerned being closed down if any of those politicians got into power. Diplomacy first, it seems, is the rule!

Normally one would say that the truth about a situation is more prosaic but I have a feeling that this time is different. I have a sneaking suspicion that the whole thing was a deliberate strategy. What better way to get everyone looking at the site and flooding Visit Scotland with suggestions for the timeline? If they had simply requested items from the public the response would probably have been poor, leaving the staff at Visit Scotland having to waste valuable time researching all the stuff themselves! At any rate, it had nothing to do with the SNP trying to rewrite history.

On a side point, history has already been rewritten as far as WWII is concerned. One contributor to the comments section of the Telegraph said that the British Empire 'sacrificed itself to try and keep europe free from fascism and tyranny'.[2] This was not what happened at all. Britain stood by and let Nazi Germany take over great chunks of Europe; Chamberlain was cheered to the rafters when he returned from Munich, remember. Even when Britain did get involved it abandoned France to four years of domination by the Nazis, while many in government were keen on coming to some kind of accommodation with Hitler to protect the Empire. Not that you will read any of this in any standard text!

The accusations that the SNP was trying to rewrite history, however, continued. At the start of 2014 Salmond and his party were accused of 'airbrushing' the 2008 banking crisis from their White Paper, which outlined the future of an independent Scotland. The document claimed that each person in Scotland would have been £900 better off under independence. The figures used, however, were from the years between 1977 and 2007, before the banking crisis happened.[10] The accusation was that the SNP was being duplicitous with Scottish voters.

The figures for 1982 to 2012 showed that each Scot would have been worse off to the tune of £2,500 if Scotland had been independent. Alex Salmond was accused of picking and choosing which statistics to present in order to make his case look better.[11] The SNP responded by saying, 'We were looking at long-term trend, and the long-term trend omits that volatile period – it is generally accepted it was a very unusual event – and it would not have allowed a fair comparison.'[12] So who were we supposed to believe?

The figures actually used by the SNP in their White Paper were not questioned but accepted as being truthful. Strangely, though, the figures being bandied about for 1982 to 2012 were not questioned by anyone on the independence side; even though they were based on a false premise. If anyone had cared to look closely they would have realised that it was the Unionists that were guilty of duplicity.

The statistics saying that everyone in Scotland would have been £2500 worse off were simply transposing what had happened to Scotland within the UK onto a hypothetical independent Scotland. It basically takes Scotland's share of the UK's debt and dumps it onto an independent Scotland. It is not, however, quite as simple as that. Those debts piled up precisely *because* Scotland was part of the UK and it is misleading to suppose that an independent Scotland would have been in the same position.

Much is made of the fact that major Scottish banks had to be bailed out with taxpayers' money. The Scotsman, for example, says, 'The financial crash had a major impact on Scotland and saw the country's two biggest banks – Royal Bank of Scotland and Bank of Scotland – bailed out by the UK Treasury after falling victim to the sub-prime mortgage scandal.'[13] Again, however, this is transposing a UK problem onto an independent Scotland and, yet again, is working from a false premise.

Both the Bank of Scotland and the Royal Bank of Scotland are no longer merely 'Scottish' banks; they are part of huge, international conglomerates with tendrils stretching to all parts of the world. Would they have grown so much and been involved in mergers and takeovers if Scotland had been independent? And would they have been caught up in all the indiscriminate lending to customers whose ability to repay was precarious? It is all, of course, hypothetical but worth bearing in mind if one is to judge how much they would have required to be bailed out if they had been operating in an independent Scotland. We are constantly told that such massive business growth was only possible because Scotland was part of the UK; it stands to reason, therefore that the risks were also only possible for the same reason. It is a fallacy to claim that the same risks would have been extant in an independent Scotland.

Even if the banks did end up in trouble it was quite possible that an independent Scotland could have weathered the storm. We have already encountered Professor McCrone and his reports on North Sea oil. (See Chapter 5) One of his recommendations was to set up an investment fund; essentially putting money aside for a rainy day. He also claimed that an independent Scotland would have been one of the richest countries in the world. With such a fund available, an independent Scotland could easily have bailed out its banks without the Scottish people suffering unduly.

That such a fund was never set up was no fault of Scotland and was solely down to Westminster. One commentator refused to see the money as having been wasted, saying that:

..billions of pounds went on public spending and, contrary to mythology, infrastructure (the Docklands Light Railway, for example, regenerated London's East End). Sure, a lot also went on benefit payments, but again it's difficult to regard that as "wasted" money.[14]

The Docklands Light Railway might have cost relatively little but it was a huge part of what is often termed 'regeneration'. Unfortunately, regeneration is a misnomer; 'Gentrification' would be a more appropriate term. In large cities throughout the world the rich are moving into deindustrialised cities and displacing the local population, who can no longer afford to live there. In London's Tower Hamlets, where the Docklands Light Railway is situated, obscene luxury exists next to some of the worst areas of abject poverty and deprivation in Europe. As gentrification extends, more and more working-class people will be thrown out of their homes and into peripheral council estates. So, really, oil revenues were used to help the new urban rich, rather than the whole population. And, as usual, London benefited more than anywhere else.

Meanwhile the rest of the money was wasted keeping millions on the dole in the cause of a political dogma. Deflation and smashing the unions were more important than the lives of ordinary people, who found their industries disappearing while they, themselves, were blamed for being unemployed. Nothing was done to stimulate new industries; all that mattered were the London banking and money-making enterprises. And we are supposed to believe that this was not a waste?

The same commentator again used the 'rewriting history' phrase when discussing an SNP referendum advertisement that compared the promises of further devolution if Scots voted NO to a promise made by the Tories in 1979. 'No vote will not kill devolution, pledges Thatcher',[15] ran the headlines back then. The SNP message was that the Tories could not be trusted then and they could not be trusted now.

Not so, argues our commentator, David Torrance. The fact was that discussions took place about the future government of Scotland after the 1979 election but the SNP refused to take part. As some of the contributors to the comments section pointed out, this was a distortion of the facts. The SNP participated in the Constitutional Convention initially but pulled out when it was made plain that Scottish independence was not to be debated. No real blame can be attached to either side: the SNP did not want to be seen to be prepared to settle for devolution within the Union, while the other parties were committed to preserving the UK. To state baldly that the SNP refused to take part, however, is a blatant mistruth.

Torrance also resurrects the old argument about the SNP helping to bring down the Labour Government in 1979. This, of course, ignores the state of the Callaghan Government at the time, limping from one crisis to the next and relying on the Liberals to keep it in power. Both the Liberals and the SNP were angered over the Devolution referendum, where, effectively, non-voters were being counted as NO voters. The whole country was crying out for a change at the time so it is hardly fair to blame the SNP for the downfall of the Callaghan Government; it had been living on borrowed time as it was.

As we can see, it was not the SNP that was rewriting history; it was the opponents of Scottish independence. Historical revisionism is nothing new; in fact, most political parties indulge in it, though it is never explicitly named as such. It is a common tactic: blaming the incumbent administration for a mess of your own party's creation. And so it was with the SNP Government in Holyrood. Labour, especially, pointed to shortcomings in the NHS, and laid the blame at the SNP's door. After all, it was the SNP that was running Scotland.

In 1997, after eighteen years of Tory rule, Labour swept into power by a landslide. It had reinvented itself as New Labour and had divested itself of many of the principles and policies that had always proved so frightening to the folk in the South of England. 'Things Can Only Get Better' we were told. Unfortunately, however, they did not.

Like most Labour supporters, I used to say that it takes a lot longer to fix things than it does to break them. Knocking over and breaking your mum's favourite vase is the work of only a few seconds; trying to repair it, or find a replacement, however, is a long, drawn-out process. And so it was with the Labour Government in Westminster.

After eighteen years of the country being torn apart by the Tories, one could not expect it to be fixed overnight.

One thing that could be expected, however, is to see some signs of improvement. These failed to materialise. Thirteen years Labour had to put things right but, instead, they were too frightened of alienating their new voters. Thatcherism was here to stay and Tony Blair emphasised the point by inviting the Iron Lady herself round to Number 10 for a cuppa and a chat.

As well as having thirteen years in Westminster, Labour also held power in the Scottish Parliament for the first eight years of its existence. Everyone expected a radical change; a righting of all the wrongs that Scotland had suffered under the Tories. It was not to happen.

Things were still running along Tory lines; deregulation and the tendering out of public services to the private sector continued unabated. No matter what figures Labour comes up with to say that it improved the NHS, for example, the real evidence stares one right in the face. Where hospitals once smelled of strong disinfectant, they now smell overwhelmingly of piss. Cleaning standards are poor and many people nowadays come out of hospital more ill than when they went in! Meanwhile, money is wasted on managers, who impose targets and want patients treated on a conveyor-belt system. Yes, the Tories implemented all this but Labour did nothing to reverse it.

Scottish Labour has the nerve to point the finger at the current Scottish Government for all this but the simple fact is that cuts in the NHS in England mean cuts to the Barnett Formula grant. Perhaps it could be argued that the SNP Government should prioritise spending better, such as abandoning free prescriptions, but it has a battle on its hands with an NHS system that has had over thirty years to become entrenched.

Scottish Labour also points to how, when it was in power, new hospitals and schools were built. What it does not advertise nearly so much, however, is how these new facilities were built. PFI was the name of the new initiative. It was a much-vaunted partnership between private companies and the public sector and it was going to save money. What could possibly go wrong?

In reality, this was not a partnership at all; it was merely a business transaction and amounted to little more than a mortgage. A private contractor would build the school or hospital and then lease it back over a long period of time and at a high interest rate. It also tied the schools and hospitals into some of the most onerous contracts this side of Ibrox![16]

There were stories throughout the UK of hospitals being tied into expensive cleaning contracts, while even minor maintenance cost absolutely obscene amounts of money.[17] Scotland, of course, was not immune to this state of affairs.

Hairmyres Hospital, in East Kilbride, for example, cost £68m to build but the repayments, over 30 years, were going to come to ten times that amount. In some cases the contractors even had a lease on the land, so that New Craigs Hospital, near Inverness is going to keep costing the tax payer for the next 99 years, while the lease on Edinburgh's Royal Infirmary is a whopping 130 years![18]

The cleaning and maintenance contracts tied in with these PFI buildings are unbreakable and leave NHS Trusts no room at all for manoeuvre. Writer and political activist, George Monbiot, explained the situation facing Edinburgh's Royal Infirmary in 2010:

This summer Edinburgh Royal Infirmary, thanks to the extortionate terms of its PFI contract, found itself with a shortfall of £70m. Under other circumstances it would suspend maintenance work and cut ancillary services until the crisis had passed. But its contract demands that it does the opposite: it must protect non-clinical services by cutting doctors, nurses and beds.[19]

And yet Scottish Labour has the gall to blame the current,

SNP, administration for the current failures of the NHS.

A case in point is Brian Wilson, a leading figure in Blair's government, who wrote in the Scotsman in December 2014:

She (Nicola Sturgeon) is seven years and seven months in, the great majority of that time with ministerial responsibility for the NHS in Scotland. So maybe it is time for her to start "taking lessons" in how to exercise a little humility and suppress her partisan instincts when called to account over the real difficulties which exist within the NHS in Scotland.[20]

Perhaps Wilson could explain how Ms. Sturgeon was supposed to have paid off a 130-year lease in seven years and seven months?

Labour seem to have become adept at forgetting that they have mortgaged the whole future of the NHS, not only in Scotland but throughout the UK. Not a big enough fuss has been made about these farcical deals that Labour made so not enough people are aware of exactly why the NHS is struggling. And yet, during the referendum campaign, Labour politicians were right there with the others, accusing the SNP of 'rewriting history'. Hypocrisy is not a strong enough term!

When it comes to history it is usually claimed that the BBC cannot be beaten for historical documentaries and dramas. It has had many successes in these areas over the years and probably expects to have equal success in the future. In an independent Scotland, however, we would know nothing about it. According to the Unionists, we would never see another BBC programme again.

11

An Empty Screen

Right from the off, almost as soon as the SNP was elected to office in Holyrood, we were told that an independent Scotland's population would have no access to the BBC. There was no reason why they should not; like the currency it seemed to be just another case of 'It's ma baw!' The SNP envisioned a new, Scottish national broadcaster, built on the current BBC Scotland. Again, however, the Unionists were ready to tell us that we would not be able to afford to buy in BBC programmes.

The figures bandied about were that Scotland would only be able to raise £320m a year in licence fees, whereas the UK as a whole raised about £3.5bn.[1] This immediately begs the question: what the hell do they do with all that money? Anas Sarwar, the MP for Glasgow Central, claimed in the same article that the BBC spent £479m a year on sports events alone. (Obviously Gary Lineker does not come cheap!) Assuming the figures used are based on the American version of a billion (i.e. a thousand million) then the BBC is still left with over £3bn. Where does it go?

Programmes like 'Cash in the Attic', 'Bargain Hunt', 'Homes under the Hammer' and the like probably cost next to nothing to make; and the shows in the evening are not much better. 'The One Show' and 'Graham Norton' are full of folk plugging new films etc. so the big celebrities they feature probably appear for nothing. And then there are the celebrity quiz shows, like 'Q.I', 'Have I Got News For You' and the execrable 'Never Mind the Buzzcocks', which will be equally as cheap to produce. There is quite obviously not a lot of money being spent on programmes.

Remember what BBC1 used to be like on a Saturday? The morning would be taken up with some extravaganza, like 'The Multi-Coloured Swap Shop', 'Going Live' or

'Live and Kicking'. Then the afternoon was given over to 'Grandstand' with all different sports being catered for. Now? It is back-to-back cookery shows, with a couple of cameras in an empty studio watching folk try to make an omelette, followed by some female batting her eyelashes and simpering at you while mixing up a chocolate cake. It makes you long for the days of the Open University broadcasts!

But there are all those different BBC channels to choose from now; BBC1, BBC2, BBC3, BBC 4, BBC ALBA, CBBC and CBeebies. They are, however, hardly full of what you would call quality programmes. BBC2 tends to be just filled with nothing but talking heads these days; somebody wandering about some building telling you its history. BBC3 is a wasteland of cheap shows punctuated with endless repeats of Family Guy. BBC4 specialises in archive shows, with bits out of ancient 'Top of the Pops' and 'The Old Grey Whistle Test' programmes, repackaged as 'Sounds of the 70s' or whatever. As for BBC Alba, there are probably more people that speak Urdu or Punjabi in our country now than speak Gaelic; so who is it aimed at? The children's channels, too, leave a lot to be desired. Come back 'Rentaghost' – all is forgiven!

Every BBC channel is wall-to-wall cheap programming these days (*pace* 'Points of View' correspondents). Some of the shows beggar belief, like 'Doctor Who Confidential'. A one-off documentary about how 'Doctor Who' is made might be interesting, but do we really need to see behind the scenes of every bloody episode? Then there is 'It Takes Two' which offers a similar behind-the-scenes look at 'Strictly Come Dancing'. At one point they even inflicted 'Eastenders Revealed' on us. Do they really think we are interested in how a programme is made? All we really want is decent shows; nobody cares what goes on behind the scenes!

But what of the quality programmes for which the BBC is renowned? Unfortunately there is very little of that to be seen these days. Drama has gone downhill completely. You do not get 'Play for Today' anymore and series like 'I Claudius' are nothing but a distant memory, as are the serialisations of classic novels the BBC used to show on Sundays. In recent years the best that has been offered to us are 'Rome' and 'The Tudors', both of which were made by an American company, HBO. Even the current hit drama, 'The Fall' is a collaboration with other TV companies, as is evident at the end of the credits.

Sport is gradually disappearing from the BBC as well. All the major horse races are already on Channel 4, while live football, rugby and cricket are pretty much the preserve of SKY and BT. Now there is talk of much of Wimbledon being on BT, while ITV is looking to snatch the football highlights from the BBC.[2] This means that Gary Lineker will be forced to rely solely on his crisps money! It also means that, soon, all the BBC will be able to offer us in the way of sport is the Oxford vs Cambridge boat race!

The point that I am rather overelaborating here is that you could count on the fingers of one hand the number of programmes you would miss if the BBC was no longer available. Even the wildlife documentaries that everyone used to rave about on 'Points of View' seem like old hat these days. When you have seen one polar bear you have seen them all and if we feel the urge to watch a good natural history programme we can always get a couple of David Attenborough DVD box sets.

A major sore point about the BBC is that much of the licence-fee money is going on obscenely large salaries. Terry Wogan gets paid a fortune to host 'Children In Need' once a year, while other celebrities get inflated wage packets to stop them swanning off to ITV, Channel 4 or even SKY. The backroom staff must get paid plenty as well; the money certainly is not being spent on programmes!

If an independent Scottish broadcaster could not do better than the BBC, it certainly could not do any worse! It would be able to do lowest-common-denominator shows along with the best (or worst) of them. How about 'I'm a Celebrity – Get me out of the Beechgrove Garden'? Or 'Sounds of the 50s' with old bits out of the 'White Heather Club'? Or what about 'Great Scottish Bus Journeys' where somebody famous can take the nearly 12-hour trip from Glasgow to Portree or intrepidly board a night bus in Glasgow to one of the outlying housing schemes? We would hardly notice the difference from the current schedule!

Joking aside, though, the thought of losing 'Doctor Who' or 'Eastenders' fills some people with dread and while many of us would rejoice at 'Strictly Come Dancing' never being inflicted on us again by our spouses, said spouses would certainly have something to say about it if one of their favourite programmes disappeared from the screen! This was the threat that Better Together was holding over folks' heads; vote YES and you will never see Phil Mitchell or Tess Daly ever again!

The fact, however, is that it was an empty threat. Even without a Scottish version of the BBC to show the programmes, all the BBC channels are available on SKY and cable. Not everybody has SKY or cable it is true but having the minimum package is actually not a lot dearer per month than the current TV licence, so it would be affordable if there was no longer the need to pay for a licence. Even if the Scottish Government were to introduce a licence, SKY and the cable companies are always willing to do special deals and it would be an easy matter for either Holyrood or local councils to cheaply organise basic cable or satellite TV for its residents.

There would not be much chance of the BBC refusing to allow SKY to carry its channels in Scotland; it is not big enough to take on Rupert Murdoch! If the BBC channels were to vanish from SKY then most people in Scotland with the basic package would not want it anymore; something that SKY would not take lying down!

Failing any of that, there was always the internet. BBC iplayer is already available to view without a TV licence, not only on computers but on games consoles and on some televisions that can connect to the internet. Noises came from the BBC that the iPlayer is 'geo-sensitive' and can be blocked if you live in certain locations. This, apparently, is based on your IP address[3] and means that viewers in an independent Scotland could be stopped from accessing programmes in this way.

Tech-speak like this can sound impressive but is actually nonsense. I have just looked up my IP address geo-location and only one site has actually got it correct. One has me placed in somewhere called New Town in Scotland, while two others have me in Manchester and Milton Keynes; two sites could only tell me that I am in the UK. I used one website that gives you the results from others and this site states, 'it is almost impossible to find exact location of a host given its IP address.'[4] Try it yourself; just click on 'Find my IP' at the top, then click 'Home' and you can find out where you really are, instead of where you think you are! The fact is, nobody can find out where you live from your IP address unless you tell them.

Even if the BBC were to find some foolproof way to discover people's location from their IP address, there are always other (whisper it) ways to watch television programmes. A quick search on Google will reveal various sites where one can stream or download the latest episodes of various TV programmes; illegally, it has to be said.

Faced with the choice of people accessing its programmes for free, whether legally or not, or making money by selling to an independent Scottish broadcaster, it is obvious which one any commercial venture worth its salt would choose. It is also clear that, since people would be able to watch programmes without paying a penny to the BBC then the bargaining position of the BBC would be significantly weakened and that of an independent

Scottish broadcaster strengthened.

So what kind of deal could be reached so that Scotland could still watch the BBC? Again, Stuart Campbell comes to the rescue with some facts and figures.[5] He tells us that RTE in Ireland paid about £20.7m for "Acquired programmes – overseas" and that, as part of this, Irish TV viewers can watch BBC1, BBC2, BBC3, BBC4 and the children's channels in their entirety. This gives us some indication of what an independent Scottish broadcaster might expect to pay.

Since the populations of Scotland and the Irish Republic are about the same, Stuart Campbell is able to extrapolate the following expenditure for an independent Scottish broadcaster:

SCOTTISH LICENCE FEE INCOME:	£300m
BUDGET OF BBC SCOTLAND IN 2016/17:	£ 86m
COST OF BUYING BBC CHANNELS:	£ 21m
MONEY REMAINING:	£193m

In fact, why be miserly? Let us give the BBC £24m, leaving our Scottish broadcaster with £190m to spend. This would allow for some investment in proper drama, which broadcasters overseas might buy. Just imagine; we could have 'River City' with CGI monsters coming out of the Clyde, attacking the café and fighting with Una McLean. I am sure America would go daft for that!

The whole idea, then, of people in Scotland no longer being able to watch 'Doctor Who' or 'Strictly Come Dancing' was nothing more than a pack of lies! The trouble was that it was really only online that folk could find out the truth; the mainstream media continued to spread the scare stories. No doubt there were more than a few voters swayed by the potential loss of 'Escape to the Country', even if it was a lie!

As we have already discovered, (See Chapter 1) the BBC was hardly living up to the ideals of Lord Reith and was biased in its treatment of the referendum. Of course, such accusations against the BBC were nothing new. Both sides of the UK political divide make frequent accusations of this sort. The Tories view the Corporation as being a hotbed of left-wing idealism and liberalism, while those on the Left charge it with being a mouthpiece for the Conservative Party. The independence referendum, however, was a different matter entirely. Throughout the campaign there was not one complaint from the Unionist side of bias being shown on the BBC in favour of a YES vote. That alone tells a story.

The only time that there was a voice of protest from the Unionist side was after the second televised debate between Alex Salmond and Alistair Darling. There were accusations that the audience was filled with supporters of independence, who booed and barracked Darling throughout the debate. As usual, George Foulkes put in his tuppence-worth, saying, '...it was not a debate, it was a rammy'.[6] Interestingly, the consensus was that Salmond won this particular debate, which perhaps explains the Unionist's charges of unfairness!

We have already encountered Dr. John Robertson, of the University of West Scotland, whose report showed that the BBC was biased in its reporting of the independence campaign. Of course, the BBC denied this, saying, 'We reject claims of bias in our reporting of the referendum in our output. Our coverage of this major story continues to be covered according to our editorial guidelines on fairness and balance.'[7] Using crude figures of time given to each side, it could be claimed that the BBC was correct in its analysis. That, however, did not tell the whole story.

Craig Murray, a former UK ambassador, pointed out how often 'the words "Scottish independence" and "warning" (occurred) in the same sentence' in BBC reports.[8] This accorded with the findings of Dr. Robertson, who said, 'Broadcasts began too often with bad news for 'yes' and, too often, featured heavy repetition of such messages over several hours.'[2]

This was the way the BBC worked; bad news about a projected independent Scotland was given, backed up by a so-called 'neutral' expert and then a member of Better Together, while someone from the YES camp was badgered about this latest development. Certainly equal time was given to each side of the debate; equal treatment, however, was another matter.

It was like a referee in a football match giving each side an equal number of free kicks. One team, however, gets a free kick whenever its attack breaks down, while the other keeps being pulled back to take a free kick when an attack is succeeding. A superficial analysis of the match would show that each side received the same amount of free kicks, negating any claims of bias or cheating. The way the BBC was working showed the same degree of cunning.

Of course, it is a journalist's job to ask awkward questions of politicians but they should be doing this with all politicians equally. It was all very well those on the independence side being thoroughly interrogated, but where were the questions about the UK Government deliberately putting obstacles in the way of Scottish independence or manipulating figures about tax revenues from Scotland? In all cases the BBC seemed to just accept the Unionist arguments at face value.

There was a reason given for this by quite a few observers: 'The Scottish independence question is much more like the european question than it is like an ordinary general election. The burden of proof is presumed to lie with those advocating separation not with those who can live with the status quo.'[10] In other words, only those that want to change things should be subjected to intense scrutiny.

This, of course, begs the question as to why there was no dissection of Gordon Brown's proposals for extra powers being given to the Scottish Government. Surely this was a major change to the status quo? And yet, the only ones that were put under interrogation about 'Devo Max' were those on the side of independence. Obviously this explanation as to why the BBC was biased is totally inadequate. It is also a clear admission that the BBC *was* biased!

Proof, if any more were needed, of where the BBC stood in the independence debate came in the spring of 2014 when the CBI registered with the Electoral Commission as a formal part of the NO campaign. Almost immediately various businesses and organisations resigned from the CBI, including STV. A spokesman for STV said:

STV is a public service broadcaster with a duty of impartiality and as such we have no corporate or editorial position on the independence referendum in September.
In light of CBI Scotland's decision to register with the Electoral Commission we have no choice but to resign our membership of CBI Scotland forthwith.[11]

Not surprisingly, those on the Unionist side questioned STV's resignation, claiming that it was in bed with the SNP. They asked why, if STV was so concerned about impartiality, it had not resigned from the CBI sooner; after all, the CBI had never made any secret of where it stood in the independence debate.[12] Strangely, they had nothing at all to say about how the BBC reacted to the CBI's move.

The BBC did not withdraw fully from the CBI; instead, preferring to suspend its membership until the referendum was over.[13] So the BBC was quite content to maintain its connection with the CBI, merely looking to show a façade of neutrality during the referendum. Suspending its membership, with the obvious intent of returning, showed that, in essence, the BBC agreed with the CBI's stance but wanted the appearance of not doing so for a short period of time.

The questions that were being asked of STV would be equally valid if posed to the BBC; nobody, however, bothered. The whole thing seemed to have become a moot point, though, when the CBI decided not to proceed with its registration as part of the Unionist campaign.[14] Rather tellingly, the BBC took this as an excuse not to suspend its membership of the CBI. A statement said:

As the CBI is no longer registered with the Electoral Commission as part of the Scottish Referendum Act, the BBC believes that it is no longer necessary to suspend its membership. However the BBC has moved its membership to BBC Worldwide, recognising that in practice it is our commercial arm that generally leads on these matters.[15]

So there we had it; the BBC, while claiming to be impartial, was a member of an organisation that even Better Together admitted was a major player in the Unionist campaign.[16] The BBC's neutrality seemed to be nothing more than a sham.

Probably the most notorious instance of BBC bias was when a report was edited to support political editor Nick Robinson's contention that Alex Salmond had refused to answer his question at a press conference in Edinburgh. In fact, Salmond did answer the question and complained of Treasury leaks to the BBC in an exchange that lasted for over seven minutes.[17] Much of the exchange had been shown on the news earlier in the day and the incident in its entirety soon appeared online, completely embarrassing the BBC and implicating Robinson in the perpetration of a lie.

Scottish businessman, Kevin Hague, a vocal supporter of the Unionist campaign, came to Robinson's defence, accusing the YES campaigners of deliberately looking for things to complain about.[18] This is a familiar argument and is the usual response from those that desperately try to cling to old-fashioned ideas that are under threat. It is an extremely specious way of attempting to counter valid criticism. And valid the criticism of Robinson was. No amount of trying to justify his mendacious report by saying that Salmond did not directly answer the question will serve as an excuse. No other politician has ever been treated in such a fashion.

There is another point raised in Hague's blog that is worth looking at. Nick Robinson asked two questions, the second being, 'Why should a Scottish Voter believe you, a politician, against men who are responsible for billions of pounds of profits?' Hague admits that this is 'a rhetorical question posed to make a point rather than elicit a response'. This leads one to ask exactly what point he was trying to make.

Surely it is a journalist's job to ask proper questions to find out the truth; not 'make a point'! Unless, that is, the journalist in question is working to some political agenda. But, then, nobody at the impartial BBC would be involved in promoting a political agenda, would they?

For many on the YES side this incident was the final straw. A demonstration was held outside BBC Scotland's headquarters in Glasgow against the bias of the Corporation. This presented the Unionist media with a dilemma: should they downplay the numbers involved or make it sound as if a rabid, intimidating mob attacked Pacific Quay? Some chose the former tactic, saying that the police had estimated the crowd at around 1000.[19] Others decided to conjure up the image of the fanatical 'cybernats' laying siege to the BBC. One newspaper screeched:

Thousands of angry nationalists surrounded the BBC's   Scottish headquarters in Glasgow accusing the corporation and its political editor, Nick Robinson, of broadcasting "lies"
and being "biased" in favour of retaining the Union,[20]

Amazingly, the article stated that the demonstration was an attempt at media censorship, akin to something Vladimir Putin might do. This was a rather strange analogy, since it was more likely to be those opposed to Putin's dictatorial regime that would be demonstrating on the streets. Calls in the comments section for the troops to be sent in clearly showed which side was the more censorial and dictatorial!

Another comment expressed succinctly the reasons why

there was a demonstration in the first place:

OK to allow 10,000 Orange lodge supporters march (with a known doctrine of intolerance and hatred, that is democracy in action, which it is of course), but where people express dissatisfaction by peaceful means, in another demonstration they are mad, bad and dangerous? Have we really come to that?[21]

Yes, we had come to that. The BBC's bias during the referendum was obvious but any voice of protest was dismissed as the sinister ravings of people that wanted to control the media. This is a tactic beloved of dictatorial regimes everywhere, contrived to convince the population that it is better off under the status quo. Better Together, the UK Government and the media, including the BBC, contrived to use this tried-and-tested tactic and the smell of a burning Reichstag tainted the whole referendum campaign.

Rather than being a neutral voice in the debate, the BBC went all-out to support the Unionist cause. Like the Queen, many people see the BBC as being an institution above reproach. This meant that its voice carried more weight than other sections of the media. That it sided with the Unionists while pretending to be a disinterested observer was as damnable as any lies told by Better Together. At least Better Together was upfront about where it stood!

As a postscript to these allegations of bias, many sections of the media were already looking ahead to the General Election before 2014 had ended. Labour's erstwhile partners in the Unionist campaign, who had derided any notion that the BBC was biased, were now openly accusing the BBC of…bias![22] You really could not make this stuff up!

One final point about the BBC from a personal perspective; a minor one but telling nonetheless. As part of the commemoration of the beginning of the First World War, BBC4 started showing one of the BBC's epic documentaries, 'The Great War'. I had been too young to see this series when it was first broadcast and only managed to see bits and pieces of it when it was repeated in the early 1970s. I was looking forward to seeing it in its entirety.

Some of the conclusions aired in the programme were out of date, such as Europe blundering into war having been tangled up with treaties, but it was an enjoyable series nonetheless. It was especially interesting, as an historian, to see footage and hear eye-witness accounts of what happened. The programme also focused on the personalities involved, rather than generalise about different nations. Then, suddenly, they stopped broadcasting it and it disappeared altogether.

There was no word of the series returning to our screens; it seemed to have just been halted after a few episodes. In what was a massive coincidence the programme disappeared just as the referendum campaign had ended. It was just a coincidence…wasn't it?

At any rate, whether we would clap eyes ever again on the BBC's overpaid stable of actors and presenters, we could hardly miss them during the referendum campaign as they, and other celebrities, begged us to stay in the UK.

12
England Expects!

Others might have already had a say but the floodgates for celebrity comments really opened on 19th February 2014. It was the night of the Brit Awards, a show that has provided us with many cringe-worthy moments, if not hours, for decades. This night was to be no exception.

David Bowie had won the award as the best British Male solo artist for the first time in a long time. He did not, however, deign to turn up to collect his award, instead sending Kate Moss dressed in one of his old Ziggy Stardust outfits. The model delivered a short acceptance speech on Bowie's behalf, including a plea from the Thin White Duke that said, 'Scotland; stay with us.'[1]

Unionist politicians were quick to make the most of Bowie's endorsement of their cause; that was, until it was pointed out that Bowie lives in New York and has not been resident in the UK for years.[2] This made his use of the pronoun 'us' rather redundant and more than a bit silly. And so we were introduced to the weird and wonderful world of celebrities that think they are qualified to pontificate on politics.

Of course, we have all become used to celebrity big-heads telling us how the world would be a much better place if only we would let them tell us what to do. Sting used to drag some poor Amazonian man round with him, who always looked as if he had been conned into it and wondered what the hell was going on, while Sting himself would tell us all how we needed to save the rainforests. Then there are Bono and Bob Geldof, of course, both of whom see it as their mission to save us all.

Usually, though, we hear about things happening elsewhere in the world; the Amazon, Ethiopia and the like. Now, however, it was closer to home; much closer. We were not being asked to put our hands in our pockets, or buy Fair Trade goods or boycott companies that destroy the rainforests; this time they were after our votes!

And so we were treated to the unedifying spectacle of celebrities, some of them almost in tears, begging us to 'stay' with them.[3] There were Eddie Izzard and Fiona Phillips telling us how we were a family. This was rather an awkward metaphor to use. The fact that Scotland cannot be trusted with its own money, but, instead, given an allowance, shows where Scotland stood in this family: a recalcitrant child! Also rather misguided was Izzard's tale of running marathons in Scotland; it inadvertently conjured up visions of another, now deceased, cigar-chomping Englishman with a penchant for running marathons in Scotland!

Then we had John Barrowman, with a faux Scottish accent, giving us no real reasons as to why we should stay in the UK, while Ross Kemp conjured up the old 'comrades-in-arms' argument about fighting together side by side. Obviously he did not think about the fact that the regiments of the comrades of those old soldiers holding the placards were long gone; victims of Westminster cuts.

Dan snow begged us to give the Union 'a chance'. What; three hundred years is not chance enough? He was followed by some woman I do not recognise, who whined about the great theatre and festivals that 'we don't want to lose.' Where did she think we were going? Maybe she thought we were all going to bugger off and 'stay with' David Bowie in Manhattan!

It is difficult to take at face value all the 'We love you, Scotland', 'You're breaking up a happy marriage' and 'How can we go on without you' stuff. It all sounded so mawkish and almost like emotional blackmail; there just had to be some ulterior motives going on behind the scenes.

The hidden reasons of some of these celebrities were obvious; Eddie Izzard, Tony Robinson, Fiona Phillips, Richard Wilson and Ross Kemp are all high-profile campaigners for the Labour Party. Although nobody in the party would admit it, there were serious concerns that the loss of Scotland would affect the ability of Labour to gain enough seats at Westminster to form a government in the future.[4] It is easy to see, then, why these particular celebrities were so desperate for Scotland to vote NO. Discerning the motives of others, however, requires a bit more digging.

A clue lies in the fact that the only pop stars getting involved with the Better Together campaign were pensioners that had long ago given up their rebellious ways. Mick Jagger is no longer the anti-authoritarian figure getting arrested for drugs possession; it is Sir Mick Jagger these days. Likewise Sir Paul McCartney; can you imagine him making an impassioned plea to 'Give Ireland Back to the Irish' nowadays? And, speaking of the Irish, there is Sir Bob Geldof, telling us all how we are better off in the Union. And it is the saintly Bob that opens the door to what the whole 'Let's Stay Together' charade was all about.

Geldof, addressing a Better Together rally in Trafalgar Square, ranted, '… we're all f**king fed up with Westminster and it's even more frustrating for us because we don't even get to do the argument that you've begun.' He then said that Scottish people should not '…selfishly resolve it amongst yourselves by taking an easy opt out clause.'[5]

So there we had it; Geldof is a UK citizen, telling the selfish Scots not to go off and leave the mess to the rest of them. That would be fair enough; except for the fact that he clings onto his Irish passport in order to claim 'non-domicile' status and avoid paying a hefty chunk of tax.[6] What was that he was saying about an 'easy opt-out clause'?

Another 'Sir' pleading for Scotland to 'stay with us' and who still manages to get into the charts thanks to the blue-rinse brigade, is Cliff Richard. He was one of those high-profile investors, back in the day, in pine forests in Scotland as a means of avoiding tax.[7] Remember all those tightly-packed pine trees over huge tracts of land in the Highlands? They were a real eyesore and served no discernible purpose, other than the aforementioned tax-avoidance scheme. Fortunately they are all being eliminated now, but one cannot help wondering what other schemes are on the go in Scotland.

In 2013 a report was presented to the Westminster Government, showing how landowners in Scotland get double benefits; they use tax-avoidance schemes while at the same time receiving all manner of subsidies for forestry, farming and having wind farms on their land.[8] The actual people involved in owning much of this land are hidden away in companies within companies within companies. Not surprisingly, Scottish Land and Estates, the representative body of landowners in Scotland refuted the claims. Nothing, so far, has been done about this report; but it certainly put the wind up the landowners.

If Scotland became independent then the SNP promised to do something about these characters, who own half the private land in Scotland. Of course, these landowners were running scared and were desperate to avoid a YES vote, which might mean that they would have to stump up their fair share of tax. A Tatler magazine journalist went to speak to some of the more visible landowners; the Scottish Lairds.[9]

'...the buggers are out to get us!' moans one duke. While the Duchess of Argyll complains that her and her husband's stately pile, Inverary Castle, 'eats money. But what if Salmond imposes a mansion tax? We're done for,' Meanwhile, the poor Earl of Glasgow has had to install 14 wind turbines to maintain his creaking, garishly-painted Kelburn Castle. It would bring a tear to a glass eye!

Dan Snow, TV historian and son of the mad wielder of the 'Swingometer', Peter Snow, was one of the leading figures in the 'Let's Stay Together' campaign. He also happens to be married to the daughter of the Duke of Westminster, one of the biggest landowners in Britain, who, unsurprisingly, owns quite a bit of land in Scotland. This, obviously, puts a different slant on Dan Snow's enthusiasm for Scotland to vote NO!

Looking at the 200 initial names that went on the open letter from 'Let's Stay Together' the most striking thing about it is that it is full of the posh and the rich.[10] This surely cannot just be coincidence. One cannot help but wonder how many of those folk that signed up are involved in tax-avoidance schemes based on land in Scotland!

Taking just a couple of names, a bit of Googling shows that they have been involved in tax-avoidance schemes before. Michael Parkinson[11] and Andrew Lloyd-Webber[12] have invested in such schemes and it is probable that many others on the list have done so as well. HMRC is currently investigating these schemes and more and more celebrity names are emerging. It is a safe bet that it was not their hearts that were inducing these celebrities to beg us to 'stay with them'; it was their sphincters, quivering at the thought of their tax dodging being exposed!

Snow and Izzard organised a rally to take place in Trafalgar Square on 15th September. The signatories to the open letter were all invited, including Paul McCartney and Mick Jagger.[13] Neither turned up but the papers were remarkably silent as to why. McCartney's reasons are debatable but it is possible to hazard a guess as to why Jagger did not appear; he is a tax exile, who can only spend so much time in the UK each year.[14] Possibly he did not want to waste his allocated days on something he would not be paid for!

There was no compunction, however, about the press telling us why Sean Connery would not be appearing to support the YES side. We were informed straight out that it was because of his tax-exile status.[15] Given the current zeitgeist where everyone wants something done about rich tax dodgers, this hardly painted Connery in a good light. It was strange, however, that the media did not deem it worthwhile to expose the truth in this way when it came to Mick Jagger! All the Telegraph could tell us was that the poor soul was abused on Twitter by 'cybernats'.[16]

Once all the 'Sirs', 'Lord', 'Ladies' and other assorted toffs and millionaires had signed the open letter, it was put on the internet for the common plebeians to sign as well. By the end of the whole campaign they boasted 115,000 signatures.[17] It seems like an impressive figure until you realise that this was all they could muster from the whole of the United Kingdom minus Scotland. Considering that this amounts to about 60 million people then only around a quarter of one percent thought that the union with Scotland was worth saving. What happened to the other 99.75%?

It was pretty obvious that the vast majority of the rest of the UK could not have cared less about Scottish independence. In fact, if anything, many people in England were pretty enthusiastic about Scotland voting YES. Have a look at some of these comments from online newspaper forums:

Bye bye Scotland. Not nice knowing you.[18]

We pay for their children's education, yet we have to pay for ours. 10% of all race discrimination cases are in Scotland against people from the UK. Let them go. They hate us, and they deserve everything coming to them. It will be cheaper for us too.[19]

Good riddance to the 41 Jock MP's say I!!!!!!
Time we ruled ourselves & no tiny minority ruled our roost!!!!!!!![20]

England pay for English and Scottish prescriptions, which is why they are free in Scotland.
Scotland gets 10% more per head of population in Scotland than we do in England, Wales and N Ireland.
If they vote yes we will have 5 million time 10% per year to offset the problems caused by independence.[21]

I'm English and I would vote YES. I hope this is our chance to get rid of this ungrateful whining country and I hope ALL the Scots go back to Scotland. England doesn't need Scotland or Wales or Northern Ireland, get rid of them all so we can get on with saving England from the EU dictators.[22]

No doubts there about how those folk felt about Scottish independence! Obviously many people in England had swallowed whole the myth of Scotland existing on handouts from the English taxpayer and, understandably, they would be more than happy to be rid of us. It certainly looked as if it would have been more in the interests of those wanting Scottish independence to insist that the English voted on it rather than the Scots!

This, of course, begs the question as to why those in power were so desperate to hang onto Scotland. And who were those 115,000 people extending the hand of friendship, hoping that we would vote NO? There is a ready-made PhD thesis waiting for some future historian, investigating the demography of the 'Let's Stay Together' letter signatories. It would be interesting to find out just what their motives were and if they were the same as all those has-been pop stars and television personalities.

But it was not just the rich and famous that were desperate for us to vote NO. Apparently the whole world was keen for us to stay in the UK; and the Unionist media lost no time in letting us know how all the world's leaders supported the NO campaign..

13

The Man from Crimea, He say, 'Yes!'

As we saw earlier, (See Chapter 8) the Unionists led us to believe that other countries with separatist movements within their borders were against Scottish independence. There was no way of knowing, however, since the leaders of said countries kept their mouths shut by-and-large. Other world figures were not quite so reticent about backing one side or the other in the referendum campaign.

First, however, let's have a look at the ones supporting Scottish independence out there in the big, bad world; or, at least, the ones that the Unionist press claimed were supporting Scottish independence. The main supporter, and the one that frightened the Establishment the most, was, apparently, Russia.[1] Vladimir Putin and the Kremlin supposedly saw Scottish independence as providing an excuse for their support for separatist movements in Ukraine.

The situation in Ukraine shows the hypocrisy of international realpolitik at its very worst. It looks as if Putin is trying to unite all ethnic Russians into the Russian Federation[2] and the West is constantly making comparisons to Nazi Germany and the Anschluss. When Russia got involved in Crimea the powers-that-be in Moscow pointed to the referendum there that had called for secession from Ukraine. The Western Powers, of course, denounced the referendum as being rigged.[3]

Putin always points to events in Kosovo in the 1990s as evidence of the West's hypocrisy when it comes to separatist movements. When ethnic Albanians fought against the then Federal Republic of Yugoslavia to attain independence, NATO joined in on the Kosovan side without the approval of the UN. No real condemnation was forthcoming and everyone fell over themselves to recognise Kosovan independence.[4] There was no hesitation either in recognising Montenegro when it, too, broke away, leaving Serbia on its own.[5]

With separatist upheavals taking place in the Eastern Ukraine regions of Donetsk and Luhansk and the Western Powers standing firm against them, it is beginning to look like a new Cold War is in the offing. As with the last Cold War, the two main protagonists will make diplomatic noises at each other while fighting one another by proxy in other areas. Any nation is fair game to be used as a pawn in these power games and Scotland fitted the bill perfectly. A stage-managed show of support for Scottish independence took place in Donetsk,[6] and there were stories in the right-wing press of a 'domino effect' in Europe if Scotland became independent.[7]

This was the rhetoric used by the USA during the Cold War with the Soviet Union and seems to confirm the notion of a new Cold War with the Russian Federation. Meanwhile, another of those ubiquitous, right-wing think-tanks, the Gatestone Institute, published a piece warning how Western Europe would be too weak to stand up to Putin if Scotland became independent.[8]

Battle lines were being drawn and those in Scotland that espoused independence were being depicted as traitors to a righteous cause. Many of us were brought up with the image of the Russian as the bogeyman so it was a powerful figure of fear to conjure. Meanwhile, the Russians were painting a different picture of people being denied their democratic rights. Scotland was caught in the middle and effectively being told that a vote for independence was a vote for the domination of Europe by the Russians.

As if to compound these old-fashioned, Cold-War arguments the Unionist press also told us the ridiculous story that Kim Jong-Un, dictator of North Korea, was supporting Scottish independence![9] Since it is virtually impossible to get accurate information about what is going on in North Korea it was rather unlikely, to say the least, that the reports were true. It certainly showed that the bottom of the Unionist barrel was being scraped with desperate fingernails! Still, it helped to bring together the depiction of Alex Salmond as a mad dictator with the stories that the UK's enemies were all in favour of Scottish independence.

Such summoning of Cold-War ghosts helps to explain the support for a NO vote that came from President Obama. While stories emerged of the UK Government requesting a statement from the President,[10] the fact is that that the head of the most powerful nation on Earth was hardly going to do anyone's bidding unless he believed what he was saying himself. His call for the UK to remain 'a strong, robust, united and effective partner'[11] certainly seemed to imply that he was buying into the Cold-War 'domino-theory' nonsense.

The same explanation was probably behind Hillary Clinton's support for a NO vote. Considering she is expected to put herself forward as a Democratic candidate for the 2016 presidential election, she would obviously need to be seen to be strong internationally; there is no way a 'dove' will ever be elected US president. She said that the special relationship between the USA and the UK was 'worth everything to me and to our country.'[12] One wonders if she would be saying the same thing to the staunchly Democratic Irish-Americans if it were Ulster voting on whether to remain in the UK!

And it was not only the Americans that the Unionists were asking for support. It transpired that the Scotland Office had been in touch with embassies throughout the world to ask them to speak out against Scottish independence. And not only that; the Westminster Foreign Office met with foreign diplomats to brief them against Scottish independence.[13] Whatever promises, threats or disinformation were given to these various embassies it must be said that the tactic proved to be a resounding failure. Not many world leaders actually rallied to the call, although noises emanated from Berlin that Angela Merkel and her associates were keen to see a NO vote.[14] This, however, was so there would be more chance of the UK remaining in the EU; something that many Unionists were opposed to. No wonder they did not broadcast this German support for the Union too loudly!

Probably the biggest coup, according to the Unionists, was the implicit support given to their campaign by none other than Pope Francis. He said, 'There will be cases that are just and others that are unjust, but the secession of a nation without a history of forced unity has to be handled with tweezers and analysed case by case.'[15] Our friends in Better Together immediately claimed that the Pope was obviously talking about Scotland, even though there were many other places he could have meant.

The Guardian, rather incredibly, said in the same article that the 'pope's (sic) cautious intervention will be seen to have huge significance for Roman Catholics in Scotland, where they make up 17% of the population'. It seems that nobody has told them that the days of Roman Catholics voting *qua* Roman Catholics are long gone in Scotland; and everywhere else, for that matter. Scottish Catholics would not be swayed by anything the Pope was supposed to have said. On the other hand, some wags could not help but speculate on how the Pope's claimed support for the Union might affect the Orange Order's enthusiasm for a NO vote!

To be honest, though, the Pope's speech was like some pronouncement from the Delphic Oracle and one could read into it whatever one wanted. Better Together was clutching at straws with this one and showed remarkable naivety in believing that those of Scotland's Catholics that supported independence would rush *en masse* (no pun intended) to the NO camp.

The next source of support for the Unionists was not quite so inscrutable; indeed it was most explicit in its opposition to Scottish independence. It also came as a huge surprise.

Li Keqiang, the Premier of China, visited London in June 2014. He visited the Queen and spoke with ministers before getting down to the nitty-gritty of the real purpose of his sojourn: discussing trade and investment agreements with David Cameron. At a press conference with the UK Prime Minister, Mr Li said:

We welcome a strong, prosperous and united United Kingdom. I believe that the United Kingdom can stay at the forefront of leading the world's growth and development and continue to play an important and even bigger role.[16]

It has to be said that the Premier of China supporting a NO vote was hardly a feather in the Unionists' cap. China's record in human rights is appalling; in fact, it is one of the most repressive regimes in the world. As was usual when it came to the Unionist cause, however, it all came down to money. The Chinese Premier signed numerous trade agreements with David Cameron, worth somewhere in the region of £14bn.[17] Nobody in Scotland was going to vote NO on the word of the Chinese leader, but, as far as the Unionists were concerned, they might think twice about missing out on a share of that £14bn and the rest of China's planned investment in the UK!

Why, however, should the leader of a powerful and burgeoning nation like China bother with what is going on in the UK? Rather incredibly, the UK Government is going to allow China to build, own and operate nuclear power stations in Britain.[18] All that is required at time of writing is the Chinese designs being approved by British regulators.[19] No doubt some kind of quid-pro-quo agreements, involving speaking out against Scottish independence, were made behind the scenes!

Perhaps the most ridiculous case of a world leader getting embroiled in the Unionist cause was that of Vladimir

Putin. The Unionist press, remember, was keen to tell us that Moscow was all for a YES vote in order to legitimise Russian interference in Ukraine. And yet, in January 2014, Putin appeared to speak up for the UK when interviewed on the BBC's 'Andrew Marr Show'.[20]

This was a recommendation that was hardly worth boasting about; another repressive regime opposing Scottish independence. And yet, it seemed that the UK Government had asked for this intervention. The Russian news agency, Itar-Tass, had reported earlier in January that the UK Government had been in touch with world leaders, including Putin, to persuade them to oppose Scottish independence.[21] Of course, Downing Street denied all knowledge of this but, as we saw earlier in this chapter, they were lying.

The UK Government did get in touch with the leaders and embassies of various nations around the world; its requests for support, however, fell mostly on deaf ears. Only three world figures bothered to explicitly do as they were asked: Barrack Obama, Hillary Clinton and Li Keqiang. It was to the other world leaders' credit that they either refused to get involved or were equivocal in any statements that they made. Perhaps they were put off by the underhand nature of the requests. At any rate, the Unionists' sneaky ploy did not gain them much in the way of support, credit or even dignity.

There were other issues that came to light through these statements of support for the Union, especially that of the Chinese Premier. As we saw earlier, (See Chapter 6) Westminster claimed that, if Scotland became independent, no more ships could be built for the Royal Navy in Scottish shipyards. There were concerns expressed about the security implications of warships being built in what would be effectively a foreign country. It seemed, however, that any security implications of allowing a Communist dictatorship to construct, own and operate at least one nuclear power station in the UK were being completely ignored!²²

Persuading the panjandrums of Beijing to oppose Scottish independence also made a complete mockery of the claims that Kim Jong-Un was all for a YES vote. Such claims were obviously intended to show how evil Alex Salmond and the SNP were; obviously they were to be known by the company they kept! And then Li Keqiang was paraded with his words of support for the Union. It is debatable which regime is more repressive and inhumane: that of China or that of North Korea. The best price you could get at a bookies for either of them would be even money!

Perhaps the Westminster Government, or, at least, the Tories, would have us believe that China is now under a benevolent regime. Certain visitors to Britain, who have been welcome guests before, might give the lie to this impression. I guess, as they say, the Dalai Lama's arse is out the window now; unless, of course, he suddenly produces billions of pounds that he wants to invest!

There was one more group of foreigners that some Unionist commentators claimed supported Scottish independence. At least, this group was mostly composed of foreigners but there were known to be at least a few British people in their midst. This group supposedly had its own agenda for supporting a YES vote. The claim that this group was on the side of Scottish independence was one of the lowest, most disgusting points of the Unionist argument. It was so horrible that no official Unionist spokespeople, including Better Together, even mentioned it. The media just ignored it as it was just too despicable a slur to cast on the independence campaign. One Scottish newspaper, however, decided that it was something that we all needed to know.

14
Kooks and Spooks

Remember Spangles? Nobody really thought about them for years until it began to be pointed out that they had disappeared. The Sunday Post is like that; it is one of those institutions that is always there and always has been. Practically every house in the country used to have the Sunday Mail and the Sunday Post on the Sabbath. It was part of Sunday, like going to church, eating bacon and eggs, visiting your grandparents and your dad trying to cure his hangover with a bottle of Irn Bru.

Billy Connolly used to swear blind that nobody actually reads the Sunday Post. You just had it in the house because it was the done thing; a bit like kids with Harry Potter books. But they must have read it, otherwise they would not have been able to get the jokes he used to make about the Nature Man and the like.

I have not looked at a Sunday Post for years but I would imagine that it has not changed much. Even as a child in the 1970s there was something nostalgic and almost comforting about it. Looking at the Sunday Mail and then the Sunday Post it was difficult to bear in mind that they were both talking about the same country. The Post seemed to be trapped in the 1930s, when working folk knew their place, when people slept three or four to a bed in their parents' house and the 'meenister' would come round to visit. It probably seemed old-fashioned even to folk reading it in the 1930s!

I used to work in a museum at the top of a Victorian primary school in Edinburgh, where we found an old cooking range hidden behind a hardboard panel. There were old newspapers stuffed up the chimney to stop the wind blowing down and when we removed these they were from old Sunday Posts from the 1950s. There was the 'HON man', the 'Doc Replies', Francis Gay and, of course, Oor Wullie and the Broons. This was in the 1980s and if I had bought a new Sunday Post and compared it with the ones from the 1950s there would not have been a lot of difference.

The Post has always been conservative, both with a small and a capital 'c' and, in some ways, this has always been part of its charm. Reading it was always like watching an old, black-and-white British movie from way back; 'Goodbye Mr. Chips', 'The 39 Steps' or the Basil Rathbone and Nigel Bruce 'Sherlock Holmes' films. It made you feel nostalgic for a time you never experienced and which actually never existed. Life back in those days was sheer hell for most people and was not the happy, cosy environment painted by the Sunday Post.

Given its overall ethos, it did not need a crystal ball to predict which side the Sunday Post was going to come down on during the independence referendum. It did, however, manage to surprise almost everyone with one of the stories it printed to highlight the dangers of Scottish independence.

The article has disappeared from the Sunday Post's website but it is possible to still read it on the Tartan Army Message Board.[1] A character called Anthony Glees, Professor of Politics and Director of the Centre for Security and Intelligence Studies at the University of Buckingham, made the tired, old point of how the UK would be weakened on the world stage if Scotland became independent.

One of the UK's big selling points in remaining together is the strength of the UK on the world stage – their sword and shield. If they can no longer strike hostile forces who attack their citizens, the UK is clearly in danger of being a spent force heading towards division. And a weakened UK is exactly what the ISIS wants.

Jings! Crivvens! Help ma boab! The Post was going over

old ground here; except it was not. There was a new, disgusting and shocking twist to this story. It concerned David Haines, a Scottish aid worker, who had been kidnapped by Islamic fundamentalists over a year before. He had recently been shown in an ISIS video where the threat was made to behead him. Glees offered his interpretation of what was going on.

ISIS are masters of propaganda and realise the impact of selecting a Scot. They will hope by showing the UK is weak and unable to defend its citizens it will drive Scots to embrace independence…Islamic State are pretty cute about how we work in the West. The people who run their propaganda and online operations are probably aware of the referendum.

He then conjured up the spectre of British-born Muslims going to join Islamic State. 'It has moved from being a distant foreign conflict to a Brit potentially committing horrific crimes on another Brit.'

Essentially, what he was saying, and what the Sunday Post was reporting, was that ISIS was ready to show possibly an English Muslim beheading a Scotsman to make people in Scotland vote YES. In effect, the independence referendum was directly responsible for the murder of David Haines. And who had called the referendum? Alex Salmond and the SNP, of course; so, really, the finger of blame was pointing at them. The Scottish Government were accessories to the murder of David Haines.

No other media outlet touched this story and nobody at Better Together highlighted it. They were all quite prepared to stoop low and fight dirty; but not as dirty as this. The Sunday Post had crossed a line and the management and editorial staff should be thoroughly ashamed of themselves. No wonder they have removed the article from their website! As for Anthony Glees; this disgusting accusation was par for the course.

Anthony Glees studied German and History, gaining a doctorate at Oxford. His research interests included human rights abuses in East Germany, particularly the work of the Stasi, the state police.[2] In 2003 he published a book, called, 'The Stasi Files: East Germany's Secret Operations Against Britain'. There have been scathing criticisms of the book, especially, understandably, from those that Glees, either directly or indirectly, accused of being Stasi agents in Britain.[3] Even ex-Stasi agents find Glees's conclusions ridiculous.[4] This has not, however, dented Glees's reputation, especially in the right-wing media.

Perhaps a telling quote comes, rather inadvertently, from journalist Anne McElvoy. While discussing what Glees had discovered about her from the Stasi Files with an ex-Stasi analyst, she was told:

'Oh don't be too flattered, they (the Stasi) were trying to show they had got close to you and knew you to please their superiors.'[5] In other words, one cannot put too much faith in the truth of what is contained in the files compiled by the Stasi. Glees, however, seems more than happy to do so. The reason why is perhaps shown in another quote from the professor. When he took up his new post at Buckingham University in 2008, he took umbrage at the suggestion that the place was Thatcherite. He said, 'If there's one-dimensional politics in British higher education, it's a left-of-centre to Marxist consensus in the state system.'[6] He obviously saw some kind of socialist conspiracy in place and was resorting to McCarthyite attacks.

Many of the academics and politicians attacked in Glees's book are accused of being woolly-headed Marxists that were easily used by the cynics of Stasi. In 2005 he published a report, promoting virtually the same theme, called, 'When Students Turn to Terror: How safe are British universities?' This time he was claiming that universities in the UK were ideal breeding grounds for extremism, from animal rights activists to Islamic fundamentalism and even the BNP.[7]

This report was commissioned by right-wing think-tank, the Social Affairs Unit, which, from its publications, is pretty much obsessed with Islam and immigrants.[8] A bit like Glees himself.

It seems to have been around this time that Glees was touted as an 'expert in terrorism' and started appearing as such in the media. Not surprisingly, it was mostly the right-wing press that accepted everything that he had to say unquestioningly. An example is an article in the Telegraph by Ruth Dudley Edwards, which, five years after Glees's report came out, was propounding the same ideas.[9]

Ruth Dudley Edwards, whom we have already met (See Chapter 3) is, as well as being an historian and a novelist, an apologist for English involvement in Ireland and for the Ulster Unionists. She was also involved in another right-wing think tank, the Centre for Social Cohesion. This group was eventually absorbed into the Henry Jackson Society, with which we have also become familiar. (See Chapter 6) Rather strangely, the Telegraph describes her as an 'Islamic specialist' when she is actually nothing of the sort.

Of course, the world of academia did not take this lying down, questioning Glees's methodology and accusing him of jumping to conclusions by selective use of his sources (one of the worst accusations you can make against an historian).[10] Despite this, folk in authority still insisted on believing every word he said. Muslim students were harassed by the security services, including Tayside Special Branch infiltrating student meetings at Dundee University.[11]

Glees was to go even further in trying to blame academic institutions for Islamic fundamentalist extremism; he called for grants to be removed from universities and colleges that refused to spy on their students. The Daily Express, of course, agreed with him, using the headline, 'Lee Rigby 'colleges' of hate face financial penalties'.[12] Of university authorities Glees had this to say in the article:

'The trouble is some are so terrified of not being

171

welcoming to all their students they simply don't dare ban extremists.'

Glees also made great play of the amount of funding that apparently came from the Middle East into UK universities. The fear of losing this funding, according to him, means that universities will not speak out. He said that, 'those within our great universities who are deeply anxious about these developments keep their counsel and will only ever speak "off the record".'[13]

Now that sounds vaguely familiar; where have we heard it before? It was one of the claims constantly made by Better Together during the referendum campaign. Remember how we were told that many business leaders in Scotland were too scared to support a NO vote for fear of a backlash from the Scottish Government? And the same claim was made about Scottish academics.

At the risk of sounding like Professor Glees, it would appear that Better Together was being advised on strategy by one or more of these right-wing think tanks. If not, it was a remarkable coincidence that the Unionist campaigners were using the exact same modus operandi as Anthony Glees and his fellow extremists. It was a clever way to go about things; there was no way that anybody could prove that they were lying, even if they were. It is difficult to imagine the bumbling, clod-hopping Better Together campaigners coming up with this idea on their own!

This probable involvement of right-wing think tanks in the Better Together campaign raises the spectre of a more sinister prospect; the involvement of the UK security services.

MI5 has been involved for years in Northern Ireland, ostensibly acting in a counter-terrorist capacity. In reality, however, there was collusion with Loyalist terrorist groups, showing that security came a distant second to politics.[14] The UK Government even had to apologise for MI5's involvement in murder.[15] Not that MI5 had been overly concerned about morality; its agents used torture frequently in Northern Ireland and even taught their techniques to foreign dictators.[16]

The rest of us were not left out of MI5's machinations either. At one point it had secret files on 272,000 British citizens; and those are just the files we have found out about.[17] And, if Peter Wright's book 'Spycatcher' is to be believed, MI5 was also involved in trying to influence general elections in the UK.[18]

MI5 was involved in anti-trades union activities, especially against the NUM during the miners' strike[19] and there are serious concerns over its continued operations in Northern Ireland.[20] It would be surprising if MI5 was not involved in the independence referendum in some way!

Recent revelations about MI5 using blackmail to force high-level members of the Provisional IRA into becoming double agents[21] are casting the Troubles in a new light. Such double agents as Joe Cahill were above prosecution no matter what activities they were involved in. This is leading some to suggest that MI5 actually ran the Republican organisations and was, ultimately, responsible for all the bombings and shootings that were carried out;[22] this was in order to undermine the Irish Nationalist cause.

This scenario was possibly not as far-fetched as it first appears. Enoch Powell was utterly convinced that Airey Neave was not killed by Irish Republicans but by British and American security service agents.[23] It certainly seemed unbelievable that a small, breakaway group, like the INLA, could go into the House of Commons car park and, unseen, attach a device to Neave's car. The sophistication of the device also suggested the involvement of someone else. Rumours abound that Neave was intending to clean up the security services, which has led some to believe that was why he was murdered.[24]

The same rumours kept circulating about the murder of Lord Mountbatten. Stories have been rife, right from the time of his death, that the Establishment wanted him dead for some reason. One possible reason for wanting him out of the way was that he was apparently in favour of a united Ireland.[25]

Some folk believe that MI5 is still running Republican groups in Ulster and Eire; most notably the dissident groups that are looking to upset the Peace Process.[26] Whatever the truth of these allegations it cannot be denied that certain members of Republican groups had a blind eye turned to their activities. Whatever one's view of the IRA or the Provisional IRA, it is the view of the British people that counts in this respect; and it was plain that they considered these people to be terrorists. And, yet, MI5 was protecting these individuals from prosecution because they were providing information. It would appear that MI5 is not above getting down and dirty to safeguard the Establishment. Why would they not get involved in the independence referendum?

As early as June 2013 Margo MacDonald was calling on Westminster to ensure that MI5 stayed out of the referendum.[27] It seemed, however, that her pleas went unheeded since Jim Sillars was complaining a year later that MI5 *was* getting involved. In fact, he claimed to know of one agent that had already arrived in Glasgow.[28] But how was MI5 operating? What was it doing to undermine the independence campaign?

MSP Christina McKelvie offered an explanation. The online abuse that JK Rowling suffered, which was laid at the door of the 'cybernats', appeared to have been the work of only a few people. None of the accounts involved could be traced back to YES campaigners and one even turned out to be the hacked account of an Edinburgh-based charity. It was all highly suspicious and McKelvie suggested that the whole thing had been orchestrated by MI5 agents provocateurs.[29]

The very idea was poo-pooed by Westminster, while Michael McMahon, a Labour MSP, said, 'The nationalists are really starting to lose touch with reality. First Jim Sillars

174

said MI5 was out to get them, now Christina McKelvie blames the Secret Service for the awful abuse directed at JK Rowling by nationalists.'[30] (One cannot help but wonder if McMahon dismisses the claims in Peter Wright's book concerning Harold Wilson as summarily as he dismisses this!) It was possible, however, that Christina McKelvie's assertions were not as far-fetched as they seemed.

For decades many senior members of the SNP were convinced that they, and their party, had been under surveillance by the British security service. Of course, this was always denied but, eventually, in 2007, papers were released that showed that all the suspicions had been completely justified. MI5 and Special Branch agents had infiltrated the SNP in the 1950s in order to undermine support for Scottish independence.[31] Was it beyond the realms of possibility that MI5 had continued, and still continues with this operation?

MSP Alex Neil said:

It does not surprise me in the least to have it confirmed that the UK Government has used dirty tricks against the SNP in the past. I would certainly not discount the idea that the British state is still acting to undermine the SNP, especially given the substantial progress it has made recently. We need to get clear assurances from Westminster that nothing is being done to undermine the democratic wishes of the Scottish people.[32]

The Home Office replied that, 'We neither confirm nor deny operational matters.'[33]

So no assurances were forthcoming and we will probably have to wait another fifty years to find out that Christina McKelvie was right, just as those SNP members were back in the 1950s. There was one aspect of the meddling of the security services, however, that we did not have to wait too long to discover.

It cannot have escaped the reader's notice, or the notice of anyone that paid attention during the referendum, that the vast majority of articles supporting independence were online. The printed media, as well as the broadcast media, was almost completely on the side of the Unionists. The Sunday Herald was supposedly on the side of independence but it hardly set the heather on fire, did it? The only way to find out the truth of what was going on from the aspect of the YES campaign was on social media.

In October 2014 Keith Bristow, head of the UK National Crime Agency, demanded total access to private e-mails and social media.[34] In November 2014 Robert Hannigan, the new director of GCHQ, wanted more cooperation from the likes of Twitter and Facebook to get information about militant groups.[35] Prior to this, in June of the same year, the Home Secretary, Theresa May, called for a change in the law to give security services the powers that Bristow and Hannigan were demanding.[36]

Ostensibly these measures were to combat terrorism and to help the police combat crime. May said that bringing in such laws were a 'matter of life and death' and appealed to everyone's worst fears by claiming that:

Over a six-month period the National Crime Agency alone estimates that it has had to drop at least 20 cases as a result of missing communications data. Thirteen of these were threat-to-life cases in which a child was assessed to be at risk of imminent harm.[37]

It would be all well and good if this access to social media was confined to tackling terrorist groups and paedophile rings but May and the security services were looking for unlimited access to everything. The information gathered would only be used, we were told, to combat crime and in the interests of national security; but who decides what poses a threat to national security? Essentially the whole internet would be open to these autonomous organisations, which make their own rules and have a history of undermining trades unions, student campaigns and any other groups or individuals that they disagree with politically.

It was surely more than a coincidence that Theresa May was shouting about the urgent need for these powers right at the time when the independence campaign was gathering momentum. And the fact that nearly 45% of the people that voted chose independence probably frightened the Establishment to its very core. Obviously, just like in the 1950s, MI5 was going to have to go all-out to undermine this growing movement for independence. And where was the growth of this movement based? On social media, of course!

It was not just the security services that could use dirty tricks; politicians are renowned for it. The referendum was to provide a blatant example of this when Unionist politicians actually broke the law in their desperation to counter the growing YES vote.

15

Cheaters Together

At the start of 2012 there was intense speculation about what the referendum questions were going to be and when the vote was going to be held. There were stories that Westminster would set a time limit on when the actual referendum would take place and that David Cameron would insist on the ballot paper only asking a straightforward YES/NO question.

Cameron said that he wanted the referendum to be 'legal, fair and decisive'.[1] The final word in that statement was the most important as far as Cameron, and, indeed, Westminster, were concerned. They wanted a definitive answer; one that would settle the question once and for all and, hopefully, settle the SNP's hash for good.

There was also an urgent need, as far as the Unionists were concerned, to hold the referendum as soon as possible. Johann Lamont said:

It's necessary for the people of Scotland to be given the opportunity to decide their constitutional future sooner rather than later in order that the uncertainty around the economy, around business and all the rest of it is addressed.[2]

Those that supported a continuation of the United Kingdom were probably looking at the opinion polls that were taken during the 2011 Alternative Vote referendum.[3] The initial polls when the referendum was announced showed a large majority in favour of change. As time went on, however, the situation altered and support for the status quo had taken the lead.

The reasons for this swing need not concern us; nor, probably, did it concern the Unionists. All that mattered was that, given time, voters can change their minds. The

1975 referendum had shown the same phenomenon; an initial majority for leaving Europe changed into overwhelming support for remaining in the Common Market.[4]

This was the great worry of the Unionists; that people in Scotland would have time to weigh things up and then vote for independence. Opinion polls in 2012 and during 2013 showed overwhelming support for the status quo.[5] The Unionists were desperate to get things moving as soon as possible; while they were still away ahead in the polls. Of course, they would never admit to this and couched their eagerness in other terms, terms that turned the argument on its head and put the spotlight on the supporters of independence.

Lord Forsyth, a former Tory Scottish Secretary, said of the SNP, 'They want to spend the next two or three years creating resentment on both sides of the border.'[6]

The SNP's preferred date was some point in 2014, giving everybody plenty of time to digest all the arguments before making a decision. Of course, it could backfire and everybody could become sick of the whole thing long before it was time to vote. Still, that was better than doing it almost straight away, as the Unionists desired.

There was another matter that had to be argued over as well; the wording of the ballot paper. Both sides realised the importance of this. The SNP knew that there were many in Scotland that, although not keen on full independence, would welcome more devolution of power to Holyrood. If there were three options on the voting slip then the SNP stood a better chance, since a vote for 'Devo Max', as it was called, was a vote in their favour.

There was another advantage for the SNP in there being three options on the ballot slip: it could split the Unionist vote. The Westminster parties were aware of this too, which is why they were so opposed to including any mention of 'Devo Max' on the ballot paper.

When Alex Salmond and David Cameron finally met and

signed the agreement over the referendum, it was hailed as a triumph for the Unionist side.[7] There would only be one question; whether Scotland should be an independent nation, with two choices, YES or NO. It seemed that Salmond had 'lost the coin toss' so to speak and that the advantage was all on the side of the Unionists.

When Alex Salmond announced the date for the referendum there still seemed to be nothing to worry about as far as the Unionists were concerned. All the polls showed massive support for a NO vote; support for independence only amounted to a third of voters at best.[8] It looked as if the campaigners for independence were going to have to work hard; even then they probably did not have a hope in hell!

As the campaign progressed, however, and September 18th loomed ever closer, the gap between YES and NO narrowed so much that it was quite possible that Scotland might vote for independence. The view now was that perhaps Cameron was not quite the astute politician everyone had thought; it seemed that it was Salmond that had really triumphed in the Edinburgh Agreement. Cameron had conceded too much just to keep 'Devo Max' off the ballot paper.[9]

Probably the biggest mistake Cameron made was to allow Salmond to totally control the wording of the referendum ballot. This allowed Salmond to pose the simple question, 'Should Scotland be an independent country?' This meant that the Better Together campaign was advocating a NO vote and appeared negative right from the start. If the ballot had been worded differently, for example, 'Should Scotland remain in the UK?' then it would have been the supporters of independence that would have had to campaign for a NO vote.[10]

It was now thought that it was a mistake not to have included 'Devo Max' on the ballot paper. At the time it seemed like a good idea not to allow the SNP the comfort of a 'consolation prize'; now, however, it looked as if it would have provided perhaps the only way to save the Union.[11] And something certainly needed to be done to save the Union, as polls began to suggest that the YES vote was pulling ahead.[12] There was an increasing sense of panic in the Unionist ranks.

Salvation came from a surprising and completely unlikely source. Step forward Gordon Brown, *deus ex machina*, to save the day. In June 2014 Brown suddenly appeared on the scene to speak up for the Union both passionately and eloquently. Cynics might point to the fact that he had a new book, 'My Scotland, Our Britain: A Future Worth Sharing', to plug; the fact was, though, that his speeches sounded a lot more heartfelt and convincing than any Better Together efforts to date.

By September Brown had essentially taken over as the guiding light of the whole Unionist campaign. He promised fast-tracked new powers to Scotland if its people voted NO. There were questions about what possible authority he, now a mere backbencher, could have to give power to anyone. It soon emerged, however, that the leaders of all three UK parties were rallying round Brown and his proposals.[13]

The rules for the conduct of the referendum campaign were set out in the Edinburgh Agreement and before the actual campaign took place. One of these rules concerned government and public bodies getting involved twenty-eight days immediately prior to the vote.

It is customary for there to be a period before elections in the UK, during which Ministers and other public bodies refrain from publishing material that would have a bearing on the election. Section 125 of PPERA (Political Parties, Elections and Referendums Act) sets out the restrictions that apply to Ministers and public bodies in the 28 days preceding referendums held under that Act... The UK Government has committed to act according to the same PPERA-based rules during the 28 day period.[14]

On Sunday 7th September George Osborne, the

Chancellor of the Exchequer, told the BBC, 'You will see in the next few days a plan of action to give more powers to Scotland; more tax powers, more spending powers, more powers over the welfare state.'[15] Obviously he was referring to Gordon Brown's master plan but the big question was, were he and the others in Government breaking the rules? Surely these promises of new, rushed legislation were 'publishing material that would have a bearing on the election'?

The actual rules drawn for the referendum by the Scottish Government, to which the UK Government promised to abide, included restrictions during the 28 days on 'information on the referendum, issues relating to Scotland becoming an independent country, arguments for or against any outcomes and anything designed to encourage voting'.[16] It certainly looked as if the Westminster Government was deliberately flouting the referendum rules.

Predictably, the UK Government denied that it was breaking regulations, saying that it was the political parties that were promising the new legislation, not the Government.[17] No wonder it had been left to Gordon Brown to introduce these new measures; it made it look like a Private Member's Bill and nothing to do with the Government at all.

Just over a week later, on 15th September, the Daily Record had on its front page a pledge, a vow, signed by the leaders of the three main UK political parties. On its webpage, accompanied by a picture of Cameron, Clegg and Miliband in matching suits, looking like one of those opera-singing boybands, the Record outlined what was being promised.[18] It was a bribe, pure and simple, and, as the Record kept telling us, it all hinged on Scotland voting NO.

Of course, this promise was a complete and utter disgrace. Not only were the Unionists bending the rules almost to breaking point, but the whole idea of not permitting 'Devo Max' on the ballot paper in the first place was to present Scotland with a straight choice: in or out of the UK. Now they were muddying the waters by introducing a measure that they had denied the SNP. It was, to say the least, completely unethical.

It was also unfair on the Scottish electorate. About 800,000 people,[12] nearly 20% of the voting public, had registered for a postal vote and by the time 'The Vow' appeared all the postal votes were already in. It was a ridiculous state of affairs to introduce new promises like this when a good chunk of the population had already voted.

Putting aside for a moment the moral and legal concerns, there was also the fact that the whole thing was disingenuous. 'The Vow' included giving the Scottish Government tax-raising powers while maintaining the Barnett Formula grant, at a reduced rate, of course. There would be no interference on how the Scottish Government spent its money and a crucial promise that the NHS in Scotland would be completely under the control of Holyrood. This, however, was something of a fallacy.

We have already looked at how the Barnett Formula works (See Chapter 6) and how the grant to Scotland would be affected if Government spending in England was reduced. Given the way creeping privatisation of the NHS is happening in England it is entirely possible that Government spending will be reduced, with a subsequent reduction in Scotland's grant. The Scottish Government would then face the choice of either making cuts or raising taxation; either way it would give the opposition in Holyrood a great deal of ammunition, and possibly help Labour, and maybe even the Conservatives, regain their lost power.

This was all tied in with the West Lothian Question. Many Westminster MPs, especially among the Conservatives, are more than a little peeved at Scotland having its own parliament while Scottish MPs can still vote in London on matters affecting the rest of the UK. SNP MPs might scrupulously refrain from voting in these circumstances but Labour and the Liberal-Democrats are not above letting Scottish Members take part. Would the Tory rank and file be prepared to hand even more powers to Holyrood without placing restrictions on the voting rights of Scottish MPs at Westminster?

Such restrictions might appear not to matter much; after all, does anyone really care in Scotland if our MPs do not vote on English measures? It is worth remembering, however, the effects that English spending, or lack of it, can have on the Barnett Formula. Should Scottish MPs, then, be allowed to vote on cuts in the English NHS? After all, it would have an indirect effect on Scotland.

And it was not just Tory MPs that were opposed to further powers being granted to Scotland; ordinary, English people were not too happy either. After decades of being told that the Scots were living off English taxpayers' money it was hardly surprising that plans for more powers for Holyrood just sounded like another burden for poor, put-upon England. A few of the comments on one newspaper website will suffice to illustrate their feelings.[20]

Scotland gets Devo Max and England pays. Some deal.

So Gordon Brown is going to bribe the Scots with even more English money in an attempt to keep Labour in power ad infinitum. And Cameron is OK with this? Barking. Goodbye Scotland - and close the door behind you when you go, please.

Mr Cameron. In a democracy, don't you think you should ask the rest of us, before you start throwing even more of our money at the moaning Scots?

First he (Gordon Brown) squandered the gold reserves and now he wants to further sell off the remains of the rUK to the

Scots. Can we please ship him up North and build a Hadrian Wall with gun turrets?

These were not the views of a small minority; there were, and are, plenty of people in England that genuinely believe that their taxes are subsidising Scotland and they see further devolution as just going to cost them more. Given such negativity among the voting public and MPs it might prove difficult, if not impossible, to actually get a majority in Westminster to vote Brown's proposals into law. But, then, the Unionists were probably well aware of this, which makes their vow not worth the fag packet it was written on. It is one thing to make promises; it is quite another to make promises that you know have no chance of being fulfilled.

As we now know, this promise seemed to do the trick and the Unionists won the day. That the NO vote won by a whole ten percent shows how effective this move had been; the polls had shown both sides to be practically neck-and-neck until this unethical manoeuvre was pulled out of the hat. And so the Union was saved. But what would the lasting consequences of the referendum be?

16
The '45'

Considering all the lies that had come from the Unionist side throughout the campaign, it was hardly surprising that many YES supporters thought that there was a chance of some kind of chicanery taking place with the votes themselves.[1] Their fears seemed to have been justified when videos started appearing online, showing what looked like tampering with votes at different counts across the country.

And that was not all. On the BBC's through-the-night referendum programme, Scottish Conservative leader Ruth Davidson told how a tally had been taken by Better Together of postal votes. This had been at what are called 'sample openings', where some of the postal votes are checked to see that the signatures and dates-of-birth were the same as those held in official records.[2] Nobody is even meant to look at how these people have voted, let alone keep a total! Effectively, Better Together had broken the law.

All these shenanigans inspired people to sign online petitions calling for either a recount or a new vote altogether. Tens of thousands signed these petitions within only a couple of days of the vote.[3]

As the days went by more irregularities came to light, including hundreds of voting slips dumped in a bin. Every one of these slips had the official bar code on the back and every one of these slips had an X next to the YES option on the front.[4] It was looking more and more as if there had been some kind of fraud committed.

Other explanations were given for what was seen in the videos and the whole thing was quickly cleared up or swept under the carpet, depending on your point of view. Meanwhile the police continue to investigate the business with the postal votes and the ballot papers dumped in the bin.

There were other irregularities too, including possible fiddling with the electoral register. In East Ayrshire there were stories of children receiving polling cards. One Kilmarnock Labour councillor said, after one family told her about their child receiving a vote:

…what worries me is that there are many more cases like this in East Ayrshire where families are not doing the right thing. It is also quite possible that this is not just confined to East Ayrshire and could be happening around Scotland.[5]

Many other cases of strange goings-on were reported: people turning up at polling stations to be told they had already voted, postal ballot papers without an official barcode, council drivers turning up alone with ballot boxes and no checks being carried out to ensure that the boxes that arrived at the count were the ones that left the polling stations. A blogger called 'Aangirfan' related many more irregularities,[6] which, if they are to be believed, point to a massive fraud going on throughout Scotland.

The petition calling for another vote grew and there was a general feeling among the erstwhile YES campaigners that the cards had somehow been stacked against them. Even discounting the whole notion that the vote had been rigged, there was the matter of the breaking of the electoral rules by the Unionists; not to mention all the lies, personal smears and scare stories that had emanated from Better Together. Why should those that wanted independence accept this tainted, possibly illegal and fraudulent result?

A name was coined, by and for those that felt that the fight for Scottish independence should go on: 'The 45', in reference to the near 45% that had voted YES. To them the referendum was not the end but the beginning; independence would come eventually.

Of course, everyone on the Unionist side derided this development; democracy had spoken and it was time to move on. One political commentator said, 'No one in the SNP has yet shown the ability to move on...the No campaign actually won'[7] Another pitched in with:

More than 86% of this country's voting population turned out on September 18th and the result was a comfortable majority for No. Whether or not you agree with it – and 45% of those who cast their ballot do not – I'm afraid that's democracy in action.[8]

Which, of course is all well and good. That is democracy for you; what the majority says, goes. But what if the result had been the other way round? What if YES had won? How would all those that wanted to stay in the UK 'move on'? The fact is that most of them had not the slightest intention of doing so.

Away back in 2001 Jack Ramsay, then General Secretary of the Scottish Orange Order, announced to a reporter from the Sunday Herald that, should Scotland ever become independent, 'The Orange Lodge would become a paramilitary force, if you like. It obviously implies a recourse to arms'.[9] He quickly backtracked, claiming that his comments had been taken out of context; he had been talking about a hypothetical scenario. His words, however, left no room for doubt; his organisation would not accept an independent Scotland no matter how it came about.

By the time of the referendum the Orange Order felt more or less the same about Scottish independence, although the rhetoric of violence seemed to have disappeared. Now the threat, if you can call it that, was that they would leave Scotland altogether. There was talk of fleeing to England[10] if Scotland became independent; even Wales was mentioned as a destination, which might go some way to explaining why the Welsh Assembly was against a YES vote!

There were suggestions that 16% of the Scottish population was ready to up sticks and leave if the country became independent.[11] The Express increased the scare value of this story by pointing out the loss in tax revenues that this mass exodus would represent. In the rush to exaggerate the pitfalls of independence, however, another possibility was ignored; it was quite probable that many of those prepared to leave had barely worked a day in their lives. Instead of causing a loss of revenue this exodus might well lift a massive burden from the Scottish taxpayer!

If even half of the scare stories coming from the Unionist side were true then there were many people, businesses and organisations in Scotland that were not prepared to tolerate a YES vote. If Scotland became independent then they were all going to be leaving. The Westminster Government too made it plain that it was not prepared to accept Scottish independence, threatening to mete out petulant punishments if it were to happen.

In essence, what everyone on the Unionist side was saying was that they were not going to accept a democratic vote unless it agreed with them. If the majority of Scots voted YES, those on the Unionist side were going to do everything in their power to ensure that independence did not work. And yet they were the ones claiming that we should now move on, that the people had spoken and that democracy is sovereign!

What is sauce for the goose is sauce for the gander, goes the saying and it is entirely correct. Why should 'The 45' accept a democratic decision when the other side had made it plain that it would not? It seemed that there was one rule for the Unionists and another for the people wanting Scottish independence; just as there was during the referendum.

All manner of abuse was heaped on Alex Salmond and others in the SNP, while the media gleefully regurgitated it as all being just part-and-parcel of an election. As soon as the same measures were meted out to Better Together, though, it was one of the worst atrocities in the history of the human race. We were told how the word 'Quisling' conjured up pictures of the Holocaust and the like and there was no worse insult to throw at anyone. It was okay, however, for Alex Salmond to be compared to Hitler, Mugabe and a host of other murderous dictators.

And, yet, the use of the word 'Quisling' was entirely apposite since Labour was sidling up to the Tories, not only as part of Better Together, but as coalitions in Scottish councils. Labour councillors even conspired with the Tories on Stirling Council to sabotage the celebration of the 700th anniversary of the Battle of Bannockburn.

Then there were the lies and disinformation from the Unionist side. Everybody had contingency plans; banks, businesses, even Government departments all had a Plan B in case the unthinkable happened and Scotland voted for independence. Of course, to divulge any of these contingency plans would be to admit the possibility that the other side might win. This was something that nobody in politics, or business for that matter, will ever do. And yet, there were constant demands from all quarters for Salmond to reveal his contingency plans and he was castigated for not doing so.

Celebrities lined up to beg us not to go, gritting their teeth as they glibly told us how much they loved Scotland and the Scots. The media, as was expected of them, took everything these rich people had to say at face value, asking no questions about their true reasons for wanting to hold onto Scotland. Even the Queen was dragged into the campaign with a stage-managed, last-minute intervention.

A desperate *Crann Tara* was also sent out around the world, asking world leaders to speak out on behalf of the Union. Not many responded but that did not stop the media from suggesting that half the world was terrified of Scotland becoming independent. Both Better Together and the Unionist media were especially vocal about an independent Scotland being unable to stay in the European Union. Considering that nobody in the EU had revealed anything about what would happen if Scotland were to vote for independence, any statements on the subject were pure speculation. Such statements by the Unionist camp, however, were presented as the truth, while any speculation by the YES campaigners was derided as sheer fantasy.

As well as this obvious bias, our media was also in the forefront of the myth that there was a concerted campaign of intimidation being orchestrated by the SNP; the so-called 'cybernats'. Any incident, no matter how trivial was cited as 'evidence' of this coordinated campaign. There was no proof whatsoever of the SNP organising such a campaign, but that did not stop our Fourth Estate from constantly telling us that it existed. Any abuse, or even violence, coming from the Unionist side, on the other hand, was dismissed as an isolated incident.

Calling someone a 'bitch' on Twitter was condemned as the action of a thug and a bully, while death threats against independence campaigners, and even an attempt to physically injure Alex Salmond while he was in a car, were, by and large, ignored. Independence campaigners were portrayed as bullies, vandals and criminals; those on the other side, however, were the epitome of courtesy and democracy.

All of this manipulation of the facts, though, was as nothing to the breaking of election laws by the Unionist side. There was supposed to be a period of twenty-eight days leading up to the actual vote when both the Scottish and Westminster Governments were to cease to publish material that might influence matters. The Unionists completely ignored these laws and introduced an offer of 'Devo Max' into the debate on the run-up to the vote.

Postal votes had already been cast, which meant that those voters were denied the opportunity to consider this new development before casting their ballots. The Unionists should have been concerned about this since there were many that voted YES that might have preferred

'Devo Max'. The fact that the Unionists appeared not to be troubled, coupled with the revelation that Better Together had had access to these votes prior to September 18th, raised serious doubts about the legitimacy of these postal ballots.

As we have seen above, there were other concerns about the whole vote, making many wonder if it had been rigged. The possible involvement of MI5 in the campaign lends credence to these concerns.

Whatever the truth of the legitimacy of the referendum debate, or the vote, the political landscape in Scotland had changed, possibly irrevocably. Membership of the SNP has risen spectacularly, making it now the third-largest political party in the whole of the United Kingdom. Various figures have been given for the size of this membership, but even the lowest estimate had it standing at 85,000 in November 2014.[12] It has certainly become the dominant force in Scottish politics.

Labour, meanwhile, has become tainted by its association with the Tories. Not only that, but it has lost its core electorate in Central Scotland and is no longer seen as the party of the working class. Johann Lamont, the leader of Scottish Labour, was forced to resign and said that the UK Labour Party viewed Scottish Labour 'like a branch office of London'.[13] She has been replaced by Jim Murphy, MP for a middle-class constituency, firm believer in New Labour and stalwart of the Better Together campaign. This further emphasises Scottish Labour's drift away from its roots.

People in Scotland voted consistently for Scottish Labour in the dark days of Thatcherism, which would suggest that what they wanted was the good, old-fashioned, socialist Labour Party. The party's transformation into New Labour, in order to appeal to Southern England was not what Scottish voters wanted. It was probably only the Scottish connection, Smith, Blair and Brown, which helped to keep Scots within the fold. That has gone now and we have been presented with the reality of Scottish Labour as merely a 'branch office' of the middle-class, quasi-Thatcherite New Labour.

A whole new demographic is now positioning itself in the Scottish Labour camp. Supporters of the Union are now stating their intent to vote for Scottish Labour in future, instead of Conservative (or Unionist Party, as it used to be known) as part of a tactical vote to keep out the independence parties, especially the SNP. As erstwhile Tories flock to the Scottish Labour banner, this will further undermine Scottish Labour's standing with its traditional voters.

The 2015 General Election is being touted as one of the most difficult to predict in UK history. Pundits appear to have no idea what is going to occur; will there be a clear winner or will we be subjected to another coalition? Labour does not seem to have made a lot of headway, despite some of the hated policies of the current Government. The popularity of UKIP has also thrown a spanner into the works and there are those that think that either Labour or Conservative will have to come to some arrangement with Farage if they want to form a government.

One thing, though, seems to be certain: the SNP look like being the runaway winners in Scotland. Although many Tories will vote Labour tactically, there are many in their ranks that probably could never bring themselves to do such a thing. The Unionist vote will be split, leaving the field clear for the SNP. This will obviously mean that the cause of Scottish independence will be far from dead and buried. That is, of course, unless some skullduggery is involved in the election in Scotland; but Westminster would never be a party to anything like that, would it?

Which brings us nicely to our final consideration. We encountered earlier, in Chapter 10, some of the ridiculous reasons given as to why certain English people were so desperate for Scotland to remain in the UK. We also looked at the possible, or probable, real reasons behind their eagerness to hold onto Scotland. But that was just the rich and famous; why were the politicians in Westminster so keen to hold onto what they had led people to believe was a drain on the Treasury?

The most obvious answer is the revenue from oil and gas. Despite the insistence of Westminster that there is not much of either left, we saw that there is every chance that there is plenty more still to be extracted. There is also the small matter that the Westminster Government, no matter what party was in power, has a history of deliberately underestimating North Sea oil and gas revenues. (See Chapter 5)

The current low price of oil and gas is causing a good deal of gloating on the Unionist side; how would an independent Scotland have coped?[14] These tumbling prices, however, have nothing at all to do with economics and everything to do with politics.[15] As such, the prices will be going back up sooner rather than later. The Westminster Government certainly must believe so since it has already awarded 134 new licences to extract oil and gas in UK waters.[16] Obviously Scotland's resources are still important to the Westminster Treasury.

At the end of 2014, under the 30-year rule, Government files were released that proved something that had long been suspected: Thatcher's Government used Scotland as a testing-ground for the Poll Tax before introducing it in England and Wales.[17] Evidently the voters of Scotland were deemed to be of far less importance than those in England and Wales. This perception was actually true for the Tories, who had ceased to be any kind of force in Scotland. There was no danger of losing an election by alienating Scottish Tory voters; there were relatively few left anyway.

Of course, it was not the first time that Scotland was used as a testing-ground. During WWII the UK Government decided to dabble in a bit of germ warfare so the MoD boffins did investigations into using anthrax. The island of Gruinard was chosen, even though it was less than a mile from the mainland and not very far from Ullapool and Gairloch. Nobody really knew what the hell they were doing[18] and the wind might easily have carried the anthrax spores to populated areas. Still, as long as it was far away from London, eh?

The island remained contaminated for nearly fifty years until it was eventually made safe in the late 1980s. Even then, the place was decontaminated with formaldehyde; not exactly something you would want to brush your teeth with! Thank God the Americans won the race to develop and test the first nuclear weapon, otherwise much of the Highlands would now be a radioactive wasteland!

Speaking of nuclear weapons, it was a no-brainer when it came to Westminster deciding where in the UK to posit its nuclear deterrent. The SNP, the Scottish Socialists and the Green Party promised to get rid of these WMDs if Scotland voted YES. It is rather telling that the MoD did not bother to make any contingency plans for this scenario; they probably could not. Neither Labour nor the Conservatives would dare to alienate thousands, or even millions, of voters by placing such dangerous devices in England or Wales. Instead, they all just sat with their fingers crossed and hoped that Scotland voted NO.

Faslane is only 25 miles from Scotland's largest city, Glasgow, and there are many densely-populated towns even nearer. It makes all the 'We love you Scotland' messages from those English celebrities ring rather hollow. If they love us so much then why do they not take their nuclear submarines and weapons and stick them...on the Thames?

One Englishman, in an online comments section, defied all the lovey-dovey stuff to give a remarkably prescient reason for holding onto Scotland: 'We need to have somewhere like Scotland that has stuff like oil and wood, makes things like ships, it's our last chance to pretend to be a proper country.'[19] And that summed things up quite neatly.

While Westminster has spent the past few decades turning the industrial areas of Scotland, Wales and the North of England into a wasteland, London has become a world centre for banking and finance. From being the 'Workshop of the World' Britain has gone to being a net importer of goods. The London banks make money in cyberspace while the rest of us are supposed to work in ancillary and service industries to keep the bankers supplied with the essentials of life.

Banking produces nothing tangible and it is always essential to have your currency backed with solid, tradable commodities. North Sea oil and gas have provided this backing admirably and will no doubt continue to do so for the foreseeable future. But new resources are always welcome and they have appeared in the shape of shale oil and gas.

Shale gas, however, can only be accessed by a process known as 'fracking'. Fracking, or hydraulic fracturing, is a controversial procedure, involving firing high-powered jets of water mixed with chemicals at shale layers deep underground. With even more chemicals picked up by the water as it comes back out, there are concerns that local water supplies may become contaminated. There is even evidence that fracking can cause earthquakes.[20] There was a temporary ban on such procedures in the UK until these concerns were addressed. This ban has now been lifted, even though the questions about the process have not been fully answered.

Surveys were completed in the middle of 2014 at various sites around Britain. Unsurprisingly, there was no gas found in the South of England and the report said that only a fraction of the oil reserves were recoverable.[21] (Surely Westminster was not underestimating the figures again?) The major oil reserves were in the North of England and, of course, Scotland.[22] The Queen was no doubt purring down the phone when she discovered that there would be no danger of her main domicile disappearing into a sink-hole! The rest of us might not be so lucky.

The deposits of oil and gas in Scotland are all sitting under the Central Belt, where the vast majority of people live.[23] Any attempt to get at these resources is going to put a lot of us at risk; but when has that ever deterred Westminster? That is assuming, of course, that Westminster gets to decide such things.

Remember all those promises made by Gordon Brown and 'The Vow' signed by Cameron etc.? The Smith Commission was set up to determine what powers should be devolved to the Scottish Government. The report made two recommendations that are relevant to the resources lying under Central Scotland. The first was about licences:

The licensing of onshore oil and gas extraction underlying Scotland will be devolved to the Scottish parliament.[24]

That seemed to be straightforward enough. There would be no extraction of oil or gas from under the Central Belt without the express consent of Holyrood. The second relevant point of the report was about revenues:

Responsibility for the management of the crown estate's economic assets in Scotland, including the crown estate's seabed and mineral and fishing rights, and the revenue generated from these assets, will be transferred to the Scottish parliament.[25]

That was something that was not to be sniffed at. After all, everything that lies under the ground in Britain belongs to the Crown, not to whoever owns the land. If the environmental concerns were shown to be unfounded (or if Holyrood chose to ignore them!) the Scottish Government stood to rake in a fortune. There was, however, a bluebottle nestling in this particular tin of

Germolene:

It is important to recognise the difference between 'The Crown' as a concept, and 'The Crown Estate' as an organisation. The Crown Estate is an £8 billion asset management business tasked by Parliament with managing a diverse portfolio of assets commercially and paying all profits to the Treasury. This portfolio includes the UK seabed, London's Regent Street and much of St James's, together with one of the nation's largest rural estates. It does not include any hydrocarbon rights.[26]

In other words, the oil and gas has nothing whatsoever to do with the Crown Estate, so the Scottish Government would not receive a penny from this source. Instead, all tax revenues and the buying of extraction rights would be going, as usual, straight to Westminster.

The Westminster Government is insistent that, as the Smith Commission recommended, the right to issue onshore drilling licences will be devolved to Holyrood.[27] It remains to be seen how this is going to work in practice. Essentially, the Scottish Government is going to be responsible for granting licences to companies that will be paying tax on their revenues directly to Westminster. This is obviously going to cause some trouble in the near future.

At any rate, it is pretty much safe to conclude that Westminster is determined to hold onto Scotland for three reasons: a place to keep its nuclear weapons, a place from which to plunder resources and a place to try out possibly unpopular measures. In fact, perhaps that is why the granting of onshore drilling licences is to be devolved; they might be hoping that the Scottish Government goes ahead and allows fracking. If it works out okay then the Westminster Government can start fracking away in England; if it all goes wrong then Holyrood gets the blame!

One final thought to ponder. Agreement has already been reached to let the Chinese state-owned energy company build, operate and control a nuclear power station in the UK. Would anyone like to hazard a guess as to whereabouts in the UK this power station will be built?

NOTES

Chapter 1

1. Daily Record 12-8-14

2. Our Kingdom 21-2-14

3. Derek Bateman 2-2-14

4. STV News 11-3-14

5. Derek Batman 2-2-14

6. Our Kingdom 21-2-14

7. Daily Mail 11-8-14

8. Daily Record 10-4-14

9. Daily Express 31-5-14

10. The Telegraph 10-9-14

11. The Times 18-6-14

12. The Scotsman 2-12-09

13. BBC News 23-5-07

14. The Telegraph 16-1-12

15. The Telegraph 19-4-12

16. Wikipedia: David Starkey

[17] BBC News 25-1-12

[18] The Scotsman 1-11-11

[19] New Statesman 16-2-12

[20] Wings Over Scotland 3-2-12

[21] Daily Mail 26-1-12

[22] Tribune 30-6-12

[23] Daily Mail 16-9-14

[24] Left Foot Forward 11-9-12

[25] BBC News 14-9-04

[26] Daily Mail 15-6-14

[27] Daily Mail 13-9-14

[28] Daily Record 18-11-14

[29] Daily Record 29-8-14

Chapter 2

[1] Wikipedia: Enoch Powell

[2] The Guardian 19-10-12

[3] The Scotsman 7-4-13

[4] Standpoint April 2014

[5] ibid.

[6] Wikipedia: Gavrilo Princip

[7] The Telegraph 15-7-14

[8] New Statesman 4-6-14

[9] Wings Over Scotland 5-6-14

[10] The Telegraph 13-1-12

[11] New Statesman 26-1-12

[12] Daily Mail 5-9-14

[13] The Telegraph 7-9-14

[14] The Telegraph 17-9-14

[15] Daily Mail 5-9-14

[16] The Telegraph 1-9-14

[17] Barrett's On This Day 20-4-90

[18] BBC News 16-11-07

[19] New Statesman 18-7-14

[20] Daily Mail 18-9-13

[21] Wings Over Scotland 27-5-13

Chapter 3

[1] Daily Mail 15-19-14

[2] Daily Record 10-11-14

[3] Daily Mail 8-11-14

[4] Metro 17-10-14

[5] Daily Express 12-6-14

[6] https://twitter.com/BritNatAbuseBot

[7] snp.org 3-5-13

[8] Daily Express 19-9-14

[9] Daily Mail 18-9-14

[10] The Independent 18-9-14

[11] The Telegraph 19-9-14

[12] The Spectator 17-9-14

[13] Wings Over Scotland 23-1-14

[14] Daily Mail 17-9-14

[15] Edinburgh Evening News 5-9-13

[16] Huffington Post UK 2-9-14

[17] Edinburgh Evening News 1-9-14

[18] The Telegraph 19-9-14

[19] ForArgyll.com 29-8-14

[20] Edinburgh Evening News 1-9-14

[21] Daily Mail 5-9-14

[22] Daily Post 29-6-13

[23] Daily Record 28-8-14

[24] Daily Record 29-8-14

[25] Daily Record 5-9-14

[26] Daily Express 29-8-14

[27] The Guardian 29-8-14

[28] Wings Over Scotland 19-6-14

[29] Wings Over Scotland 3-8-14

[30] Derek Bateman 29-8-14

[31] The Telegraph 17-9-14

[32] ibid.

[33] Facebook: United Against Separation

[34] The Telegraph 19-9-14

[35] ibid.

[36] reddit 19-9-14

[37] anphoblacht 20-9-14

[38] https://vine.co/v/OWPzrhni0Aj

[39] Little Green Footballs 20-9-14

[40] BBC News 20-9-14

[41] Wings Over Scotland 20-9-14

[42] Messy Reality 'Friday the 19th'

[43] ibid.

Chapter 4

[1] http://thescottishdiaspora.co.uk/?p=1111

[2] BBC News 25-5-10

[3] NASGA 24-1-09

[4] ibid.

[5] New Statesman 18-7-14

[6] Deadline 9-1-13

[7] Daily Record 22-10-12

[8] The Scotsman 28-4-13

[9] ibid.

[10] ibid.

[11] ibid.

[12] BBC News 25-8-13

[13] What Do They Know: 'Forces Day 2014 Bid'

[14] ibid.

[15] The Herald 9-5-12

[16] The Scotsman 6-2-14

[17] The Scotsman 24-4-14

[18] Scottish Government Report 23-4-14

[19] What Do They Know: 'Forces Day 2014 Bid'

[20] Scottish Government Report 23-4-14

[21] Wings Over Scotland 29-6-14

[22] The Scotsman 1-7-14

[23] Craig Murray 29-6-14

[24] Standpoint April 2014

[25] http://www.aforceforgood.org.uk/news/jm

[26] ibid.

[27] BBC News 28-9-12

[28] The National Archives: Rise of Parliament

[29] http://magnacarta800th.com

[30] The Independent 23-6 -13

[31] Daily Mail 2-1-14

[32] The Scotsman 30-6-14

[33] Standpoint April 2014

[34] Daily Mail 2-1-14

[35] New Statesman 26-1-1

Chapter 5

[1] BBC News 9-9-14

[2] The Guardian 9-9-14

[3] The Guardian 7-8-14

[4] The Guardian 9-9-14

[5] Our Kingdom 13-2-14

[6] The Guardian 29-3-14

[7] ibid.

[8] Daily Express 14-8-14

[9] The Telegraph 24-9-14

[10] Daily Mirror 9-1-14

[11] The Guardian 30-4-12

[12] This Is Money 13-2-12

[13] BBC News 25-8-14

[14] Business For Scotland 23-9-13

[15] The Telegraph 10-7-14

[16] The Independent 9-12-05

[17] The Guardian 29-5-13

[18] The Herald 10-5-14

[19] The Independent 9-12-05

[20] Daily Record 16-9-14

[21] Shetland News 5-8-14

[22] ibid.

[23] Oil Industry News 2-8-14

[24] BBC News 23-10-14

[25] Financial Times 28-5-14

[26] ibid.

Chapter 6

[1] The Herald 11-6-14

[2] The Guardian 23-5-14

[3] ibid.

[4] The Guardian 9-19-14

[5] The Guardian 31-8-10

[6] BBC News 31-7-14

[7] The Telegraph 22-8-14

[8] The Scotsman 17-6-13

[9] BBC News 8-5-14

[10] The Guardian 11-9-14

[11] The Guardian 23-5-14

[12] Parliament.UK 25-10-10

[13] Conservative Home 7-12-10

[14] Daily Mail 3-1-14

[15] ibid.

[16] ibid.

[17] Wikipedia: Policy Exchange

[18] BBC News 13-12-07

[19] Brunel University London: Academic Profiles

[20] Our Kingdom 21-2-14

[21] Scribd 27-8-14

[22] The Scotsman 29-8-14

[23] Daily Record 28-8-14

[24] The Telegraph 15-9-14

[25] Business For Scotland 18-4-14

[26] The Guardian 11-9-14

[27] The Guardian 4-9-14

[28] Daily Mail 2-7-13

[29] The Henry Jackson Society 2-7-13

[30] Standpoint March 2013

[31] http://www.georgegrant.org.uk

[32] The Telegraph 12-8-14

[33] The Guardian 7-11-13

[34] The Courier 12-11-14

[35] The Telegraph 12-11-14

[36] The Guardian 7-11-13

[37] Ayr Advertiser 17-10-13

[38] Sunday Post 6-10-13

[39] Ayr Advertiser 17-10-13

[40] Sunday Post 6-10-13

[41] University of Aberdeen: Profiles

Chapter 7

[1] The Scotsman 11-6-13

[2] The Herald 11-6-13

[3] Financial Times 23-4-14

[4] The Independent 24-4-14

[5] Daily Mirror 5-9-14

[6] ibid.

[7] What Scotland Thinks 26-9-14

[8] SKY News 19-9-14

[9] What Scotland Thinks 26-9-14

[10] BBC News 7-5-14

[11] The Telegraph 12-9-14

[12] ibid.

[13] The Scotsman: Key Topics

[14] The Telegraph 26-8-14

[15] The Scotsman 10-3-13

[16] Daily Express 11-9-14

[17] The Herald 12-9-14

[18] Daily Mail 18-2-14

[19] STV News 17-3-14

[20] Daily Record 5-1-15

[21] Daily Record 6-1-15

[22] ibid.

[23] Sunday Post 24-8-14

[24] Fullfact.org 1-8-14

[25] snp.org 12-4-14

[26] Sunday Post 21-9-14

[27] ibid.

[28] ibid.

Chapter 8

[1] Daily Express 16-7-14

[2] The Scotsman 15-7-14

[3] Financial Times 14-9-14

[4] BBC News 19-9-14

[5] Fox News Latino 17-9-14

[6] BBC News 19-9-14

[7] Financial Times 14-9-14

[8] Wikipedia: German reunification

[9] Financial Times 14-9-14

[10] BBC News 23-1-13

[11] BBC News 4-11-13

[12] The Independent 10-11-14

[13] The Spectator 13-9-14

[14] Buzz Feed News 22-9-14

[15] http://www.ukip.org

[16] The Guardian 18-6-14

Chapter 9

[1] Daily Record 19-6-14

[2] New Statesman 9-2-12

[3] Daily Express 12-9-14

[4] Daily Mail 13-9-14

[5] The British Monarchy: The Act of Settlement

[6] History Today 2-2-13

[7] Wikipedia: Elizabeth Stuart, Queen of Bohemia

[8] Wikipedia: Louise Hollandine of the Palatinate

[9] Daily Express 16-9-14

[10] The British Monarchy: Coronation

[11] ibid.

[12] The British Monarchy: Queen and Church of Scotland

[13] Wikipedia: Emperor of India

[14] New Advent: The Royal Declaration

[15] The Telegraph 9-9-14

[16] ibid.

[17] Daily Express 9-9-14

[18] BBC News 14-9-14

[19] The Telegraph 14-9-14

[20] ibid.

[21] The Guardian 23-9-14

[22] Royal Central 26-6-14

[23] The Guardian 16-12-14

Chapter 10

[1] Daily Express 12-7-12

[2] Daily Mail 19-5-12

[3] Daily Express 12-7-12

[4] Daily Mail 19-5-12

[5] The Herald 14-6-13

[6] The Telegraph 14-6-13

[7] The Herald 14-6-13

[8] The Telegraph 14-6-13

[9] ibid.

[10] Daily Express 10-1-14

[11] ibid.

[12] The Scotsman 10-1-14

[13] ibid.

[14] The Herald 18-5-14

[15] ibid.

[16] The Telegraph 16-5-12

[17] ibid.

[18] BBC News 21-9-11

[19] George Monbiot 22-11-10

[20] The Scotsman 6-12-14

Chapter 11

[1] STV News 16-10-12

[2] The Telegraph 16-12-14

[3] The Guardian 29-2-12

[4] http://www.iplocation.net

[5] Wings Over Scotland 3-3-14

[6] Daily Mail 27-8-13

[7] The Guardian 2-6-14

[8] Craig Murray 29-4-13

[9] The Guardian 2-6-14

[10] The Spectator 30-6-14

[11] STV News 19-4-14

[12] Sunday Post 20-4-14

[13] Financial Times 24-4-14

[14] The Guardian 25-4-14

[15] BBC News 15-5-14

[16] Sunday Post 20-4-14

[17] RT 12-9-14

[18] Chokka Blog (Kevin Hague) 30-11-14

[19] The Scotsman 14-9-14

[20] The Independent 14-9-14

[21] ibid.

[22] The Telegraph 5-12-14

Chapter 12

[1] The Guardian 20-2-14

[2] Daily Mail 20-2-14

[3] https://www.youtube.com/watch?v=F9qjomKLtBA

[4] New Statesman 12-1-12

[5] The Daily Edge 16-9-14

[6] The Telegraph 16-5-12

[7] London Evening Standard 21-6-12

[8] The Telegraph 13-6-13

[9] Tatler August 2014

[10] https://www.letsstaytogether.org.uk

[11] The Independent 10-2-12

[12] Channel 4 News 9-7-14

[13] The Telegraph 12-9-14

[14] Ultimate Classic Rock 15-4-14

[15] The Telegraph 16-9-14

[16] The Telegraph 8-8-14

[17] https://www.letsstaytogether.org.uk

[18] Daily Mail 20-8-14

[19] Daily Mail 31-8-14

[20] Daily Express 13-9-14

[21] ibid.

[22] ibid.

Chapter 13

[1] Ukraine Crisis 24-9-14

[2] Gatestone Institute 15-9-14

[3] The Moscow Times 19-9-14

[4] Wikipedia: Kosovo War

[5] Wikipedia: Serbia and Montenegro

[6] The Moscow Times 19-9-14

[7] The Telegraph 10-9-14

[8] Gatestone Institute 15-9-14

[9] Daily Mail 11-9-14

[10] The Independent 9-6-14

[11] ibid.

[12] The Independent 13-6-14

[13] SNP.org 20-3-14

[14] Business Insider 11-9-14

[15] The Guardian 13-6-14

[16] Financial Times 17-6-14

[17] ibid.

[18] Daily Mail 18-6-14

[19] Financial Times 17-6-14

[20] BBC News 19-1-14

[21] The Spectator 20-1-14

[22] Daily Mail 18-6-14

Chapter 14

1 Tartan Army Message Board 7-9-14

2 Powerbase: Anthony Glees

3 Times Higher Education 6-1-06

4 The Guardian 11-6-03

5 London Evening Standard 9-11-09

6 Powerbase: Anthony Glees

7 ibid.

8 Powerbase: Social Affairs Unit

9 The Telegraph 2-1-10

10 http://www.dkrenton.co.uk/glees_report.html

11 The Independent 1-4-19

12 Daily Express 22-12-13

13 National Observer Dec. 09 – Feb. 10

14 The Guardian 25-10-13

15 Daily Mail 13-12-12

16 BBC News 12-12-14

17 Daily Mail 9-7-06

[18] The Independent 28-4-95

[19] The Guardian 3-10-00

[20] The Detail 5-12-12

[21] Daily Mirror 20-10-14

[22] The Internet Post 20-10-14

[23] The Guardian 16-3-02

[24] http://www.indymedia.ie/article/104511

[25] OPC Global 21-6-12

[26] Cassiopaea 7-12-10

[27] The Scotsman 26-6-13

[28] The Independent 13-6-14

[29] The Telegraph 27-6-14

[30] ibid.

[31] The Scotsman 16-9-07

[32] ibid.

[33] ibid.

[34] RT 7-10-14

[35] Reuters 4-11-14

[36] BBC News 25-6-14

[37] ibid.

Chapter 15

[1] BBC News 9-1-12

[2] ibid.

[3] http://ukpollingreport.co.uk/av-referendum

[4] BBC Radio 4 History 18-4-02

[5] The Guardian 13-8-13

[6] BBC News 9-1-12

[7] The Week 15-10-12

[8] The Guardian 21-3-13

[9] New Statesman 8-9-14

[10] ibid.

[11] New Statesman 7-9-14

[12] The Telegraph 8-9-14

[13] The Telegraph 8-9-14

[14] The Scottish Government 15-10-12

[15] The Independent 10-9-14

[16] ibid.

[17] ibid.

[18] Daily Record 15-9-14

[19] SKY News 12-9-14

[20] The Telegraph 8-9-14

Chapter 16

1 Sunday Post 24-8-14

2 BBC News 10-10-14

3 The Guardian 22-9-14

4 Newsweek 2-10-14

5 The Scotsman 7-9-14

6 Aangirfan 6-10-14

7 Daily Record 16-11-14

8 The Courier 22-9-14

9 BBC News 9-7-01

10 BBC News 18-3-14

11 Daily Express 24-8-13

12 BBC News 19-11-14

13 The Guardian 25-10-14

14 The Telegraph 14-11-14

15 The Economist 8-12-14

16 BBC News 6-11-14

17 The Guardian 30-12-14

[18] Secret Scotland: Gruinard Island

[19] Quora: Why is England so desperate to hold onto Scotland?

[20] BBC News 13-12-12

[21] The Guardian 23-5-14

[22] The Scotsman 1-7-14

[23] ibid.

[24] The Guardian 27-11-14

[25] ibid.

[26] The Crown Estate: Myth Busting

[27] Hansard 18-12-14: Column 1541